Hiking Joshua Tree National Park

Help Us Keep This Guide Up to Date

Every effort has been made by the authors and editors to make this guide as accurate and useful as possible. However, many things can change after a guide is published— trails are rerouted, regulations change, techniques evolve, facilities come under new management, etc.

We would appreciate hearing from you concerning your experiences with this guide and how you feel it could be improved and kept up to date. While we may not be able to respond to all comments and suggestions, we'll take them to heart, and we'll also make certain to share them with the author. Please send your comments and suggestions to the following address:

Globe Pequot
Reader Response/Editorial Department
246 Goose Lane
Guilford, CT 06437

Or you may e-mail us at: editorial@falcon.com

Thanks for your input, and happy trails!

Hiking Joshua Tree National Park

38 Day and Overnight Hikes

SECOND EDITION

Bill and Polly Cunningham
Revised by Bruce Grubbs

FALCONGUIDES

GUILFORD, CONNECTICUT

FALCONGUIDES®

An imprint of The Rowman & Littlefield Publishing Group, Inc.
4501 Forbes Blvd., Ste. 200
Lanham, MD 20706
www.rowman.com

Falcon and FalconGuides are registered trademarks and Make Adventure Your Story is a
trademark of The Rowman & Littlefield Publishing Group, Inc.

Distributed by NATIONAL BOOK NETWORK

Photos by Bill and Polly Cunningham except where indicated
Maps by Melissa Baker

British Library Cataloguing-in-Publication Information Available

Library of Congress Cataloging-in-Publication Data

Names: Cunningham, Bill, 1943– author. | Cunningham, Polly, author. | Grubbs, Bruce (Bruce O.),
    reviser.
Title: Hiking Joshua Tree National Park : 38 day and overnight hikes / Bill and Polly Cunningham ;
    revised by Bruce Grubbs.
Description: Second edition. | Guilford, Connecticut : FalconGuides, [2019] | Includes index.
Identifiers: LCCN 2019007887 (print) | LCCN 2019013648 (ebook) | ISBN 9781493039074
    (Electronic) | ISBN 9781493039067 (pbk. : alk. paper) | ISBN 9781493039074 (e-book)
Subjects: LCSH: Hiking—California—Joshua Tree National Park—Guidebooks. | Joshua Tree
    National Park (Calif.)—Guidebooks.
Classification: LCC GV199.42.C22 (ebook) | LCC GV199.42.C22 J6725 2019 (print) | DDC
    796.510979497—dc23
LC record available at https://lccn.loc.gov/2019007887

♾™ The paper used in this publication meets the minimum requirements of American National
Standard for Information Sciences—Permanence of Paper for Printed Library Materials, ANSI/
NISO Z39.48-1992.

To the thousands of citizens from California and elsewhere, past and present, who laid the groundwork for protection of a large portion of the California desert and to the dedicated state and federal park rangers and naturalists charged with stewardship of California's irreplaceable desert wilderness.

Contents

Acknowledgments

This book could not have been written without the generous assistance of knowledgeable park staff. Special thanks to Joe Zarki, chief of interpretation for Joshua Tree National Park, and his assistant, Sandra Kaye, who provided an excellent review of the text. Joe and members of his ranger staff provided detailed updates for each of the Joshua Tree hikes. The effort they expended to ensure accurate information in this book is both commendable and deeply appreciated.

Our thanks also to all the hospitable folks who provided advice and insights during our treks in the desert. Please know that you are not forgotten.

Thanks to you all!

Map Legend

Boundaries

~~	National wilderness/ preserve boundary
/////////	National park boundary
:::::::::	State park boundary
~~	County park boundary
— - — - —	State boundary

Transportation

═══15═══	Interstate
══95══	U.S. highway
──62──	State highway
──S22──	Primary road
────────	Other road
════════	Unpaved road
= = = = =	Unimproved road
▬ ▬ ▬ ▬	Featured unimproved road
▬ ▬ ▬ ▬	Featured trail
············	Optional trail
- - - - - -	Other trail
┼┼┼┼┼┼	Railroad
•—•—•—	Power line

Hydrology

⌇⌇	Intermittent stream
⸰ᵒ	Spring
∥	Fall
▬	Lake
◯	Dry lake
▒	Lava bed
⸱⸱⸱	Sand/wash

Physiography

×	Spot elevation
)(	Pass
▲	Peak
∩	Cave
⊔⊔⊔	Cliff

Symbols

🚶	Trailhead
START	Trail start
❷	Trail locator
↺	Trail turnaround
P	Parking
🚻	Restroom/toilet
△	Campground
▲	Backcountry campground
♠	Lodging
?	Visitor center
👥	Ranger station
☎	Telephone
⛉	Picnic area
○	Town
👁	Overlook
▪	Point of interest
⚒	Mine/prospect
•—•	Gate
⋈	Bridge
✛▬	Airport/ landing strip

Introduction

The California desert covers the southeastern quarter of our most populous and most ecologically diverse state. Incredibly, three of the four desert subregions that make up most of the arid southwest corner of North America are found within the California desert. These subregions—the Colorado (called the Sonoran in Mexico), Mojave, and Great Basin Deserts—differ by climate and distinct plant and animal communities.

The geographer's definition of a desert as a place with less than 10 inches average annual rainfall says little about what a desert really is. Deserts are regions of irregular and minimal rainfall, so much so that for most of the time, scarcity of water is limiting to life. Averages mean nothing in a desert region that may go one or two years without any rain only to receive up to three times the annual average the following year.

In the desert, evaporation far exceeds precipitation. Temperatures swing widely between night and day. This is because low humidity and intense sun heat up the ground during the day, but almost all of the heat dissipates at night. Daily temperature changes of 50 degrees or more are common—which can be hazardous to unprepared hikers caught out after dark.

Sparse rainfall means sparse vegetation, which in turn means naked geological features. Most of the California desert is crisscrossed with mountain ranges, imparting an exposed, rough-hewn, scenic character to the landscape. Rather than having been uplifted, the mountains were largely formed by an east-west collision of the earth's tectonic plates, producing a north-south orientation of the ranges. Some would call the result stark, but all would agree that these signatures on the land are dramatic and, at times, overpowering. This very starkness tends to exaggerate the drama of space, color, relief, and sheer ruggedness.

Despite sparse plant cover, the number of individual plant species in the California desert is amazing. At least 1,000 species are spread among 103 vascular plant families. Equally amazing is the diversity of bird life and other wildlife on this deceptively barren land. Many of these birds and animals are active only at night, or are most likely seen during the hotter months at or near watering holes. Hundreds of bird species and more than sixty kinds of reptiles and amphibians fly, nest, crawl, and slither in habitat niches to which they have adapted. Desert bighorn sheep and the rare mountain lion are at the top of the charismatic mega-fauna list, but at least sixty other species of mammals make the desert their home—from kit foxes on the valley floors to squirrels on the highest mountain crests. The best way to observe these desert denizens is on foot, far from the madding crowd, in the peace and solitude of desert wilderness.

Joshua Tree National Park is in the transition zone between the Colorado and Mojave Deserts, accounting for much of its rich diversity of plant and animal life. The Mojave Desert is the smallest of the four North American deserts and lies mostly in southeastern California. Elevations range from below sea level to around

4,000 feet, with average elevations of 3,000 feet in the rugged eastern portion. Summer temperatures usually exceed 100 degrees, but winter can bring bitter cold, with temperatures sometimes dropping near zero in valleys where dense, frigid air settles at night. Plant cover is typified by Joshua trees, creosote bushes, white bursage, and indigo bushes.

Joshua Tree is included within the Colorado and Mojave Desert Biosphere Reserve, which was internationally designated in 1984. There are more than 265 biosphere reserves worldwide that protect lands within each of the earth's biogeographic regions. The parks are within the core of the biosphere reserve, where human impact is kept to a minimum. The core is surrounded by a multiple-use area where sustainable development is the guiding principle.

Joshua Tree and other desert parks receive many international visitors who are drawn to the desert because there is no desert in their homeland. Many come during the peak of summer to experience the desert at its hottest. Regardless of whether the visitor is from Europe, a nearby California town, or someplace across the nation, the endlessly varied desert offers something for everyone. Unlike snowbound northern regions, the California desert is a year-round hiker's paradise. There is no better place in which to actually see the raw, exposed forces of land-shaping geology at work. Those interested in history and paleoarchaeology will have a field day. And the list goes on. This book is designed to enhance the enjoyment of all who wish to sample the richness of Joshua Tree National Park on their own terms. Travel is best done on foot, with distance and destination being far less important than the experience of getting there.

The Meaning and Value of Wilderness

Visitors to Joshua Tree and other desert wildlands should appreciate the meaning and values of wilderness, if for no other reason than to better enjoy their visits with less impact on the wildland values that attracted them in the first place. Nearly 14 percent of California (almost fourteen million acres) is designated federal wilderness, making the Golden State the premier wilderness state in the continental United States. The California Desert Protection Act of 1994 doubled the wilderness acreage in the state and tripled the amount of wilderness under National Park Service jurisdiction, increasing from two million to six million acres.

Those who know and love wild country have their own personal definition of wilderness, heartfelt and often unexpressed, which varies with each person. But since Congress reserved to itself the exclusive power to designate wilderness in the monumental Wilderness Act of 1964, it is important that we also understand the legal meaning of "wilderness."

The most fundamental purpose of the Wilderness Act is to provide an enduring resource of wilderness for this and future generations so that a growing, increasingly mechanized human population does not occupy and modify every last wild niche. Just as important as preserving the land is the preservation of natural processes, such as naturally ignited fire, erosion, landslides, and other forces that shape the land. Before 1964 the uncertain whim of administrative fiat was all that protected wilderness. During the 1930s the "commanding general" of the wilderness battle, Wilderness Society cofounder Bob Marshall, described wilderness as a "snowbank melting on a hot June day." In the desert the analogy might be closer to a sand dune shrinking on a windy day. Declassification of much of Joshua Tree National Monument prior to its present park status certainly illustrates lack of permanency for land lacking statutory protection.

The act defines wilderness as undeveloped federal lands "where the earth and its community of life are untrammeled by man, where man is a visitor who does not remain." In old English the word "trammel" means a net, so "untrammeled" conveys the idea of land that is unnetted or uncontrolled by humans. Congress recognized that no land is completely free of human influence, going on to say that wilderness must "generally appear to have been affected primarily by the forces of nature, with the imprint of man's work substantially unnoticeable." Further, a "wilderness" must have outstanding opportunities for solitude or primitive and unconfined recreation, and be at least 5,000 acres in size or large enough to preserve and use in an unimpaired condition. Also, wilderness may contain ecological, geological, or other features of scientific, educational, scenic, or historical value. The Joshua Tree National Park wilderness described in this book meets and easily exceeds these legal requirements. Any lingering doubts are removed by the distant music of a coyote beneath a star-studded desert sky, or by a green oasis in a remote canyon.

In general, wilderness designation protects the land from development such as roads, buildings, motorized vehicles, and equipment, and from commercial uses except preexisting livestock grazing, outfitting, and the development of mining claims and leases validated before the 1984 cutoff date in the federal Wilderness Act. The act set up the National Wilderness System and empowered three federal agencies to administer wilderness: the Forest Service, the Fish and Wildlife Service, and the National Park Service. The Bureau of Land Management was added to the list with passage of the 1976 Federal Land Policy and Management Act. These agencies can and do make wilderness recommendations, as any citizen can, but only Congress can set aside wilderness on federal lands. This is where politics enters in, epitomizing the kind of grassroots democracy that eventually brought about passage of the landmark California Desert Protection Act. The formula for wilderness conservationists has been and continues to be "endless pressure endlessly applied."

But once designated, the unending job of wilderness stewardship is just beginning. The managing agencies have a special responsibility to administer wilderness in "such manner as will leave them (wilderness areas) unimpaired for future use and enjoyment as wilderness." Unimpairment of wilderness over time can only be achieved through partnership between concerned citizens and the agencies.

Wilderness is the only truly biocentric use of land. It is off-limits to intensive human uses with an objective of preserving the diversity of nonhuman life, which is richly endowed in the California desert. As such, its preservation is our society's highest act of humility. This is where we deliberately slow down our impulse to drill the last barrel of oil, mine the last vein of ore, or build a parking lot on top of the last wild peak. The desert wilderness explorer can take genuine pride in reaching a remote summit under his or her power, traversing a narrow serpentine canyon, or walking across the uncluttered expanse of a vast desert basin. Hiking boots and self-reliance replace motorized equipment and push-button convenience, allowing us to find something in ourselves we feared lost.

Have Fun and Be Safe

Wandering in the desert has a reputation of being a dangerous activity, thanks to both the Bible and Hollywood. Usually depicted as a wasteland, the desert evokes fear. With proper planning, however, desert hiking is not hazardous. In fact, it is fun and exciting and is quite safe.

An enjoyable desert outing requires preparation. Beginning with this book, along with the maps suggested in the hike write-ups, you need to be equipped with adequate knowledge about your hiking area. Carry good maps and a compass, and know how to use them.

Calculating the time required for a hike in the desert defies any formula. Terrain is often rough; extensive detours around boulders, dry falls, and drop-offs mean longer trips. Straight-line distance is an illusion. Sun, heat, and wind likewise all conspire to slow down even the speediest hiker. Therefore, distances are not what they appear in the desert. Five desert miles may take longer than 10 woodland miles. Plan your excursion conservatively, and always carry emergency items in your pack (see appendix B).

While you consult the equipment list (appendix B), note that water ranks the highest. Carrying the water is not enough—take the time to stop and drink it. This is another reason desert hikes take longer. Frequent water breaks are mandatory. It's best to return from your hike with empty water bottles. You can cut down on loss of bodily moisture by hiking with your mouth closed and breathing through your nose; reduce thirst also by avoiding sweets and alcohol.

Driving to and from the trailhead is statistically far more dangerous than hiking in the desert backcountry. But being far from the nearest 911 service requires knowledge about possible hazards and proper precautions to avoid them. It is not an oxymoron to have fun and to be safe. Quite to the contrary: If you're not safe, you won't have fun. At the risk of creating excessive paranoia, here are the treacherous twelve:

Dehydration

It cannot be overemphasized that plenty of water is necessary for desert hiking. Carry one gallon per person per day in unbreakable plastic screw-top containers. And pause often to drink it. Carry water in your car as well so you'll have water to return to. As a general rule, plain water is a better thirst-quencher than any of the colored fluids on the market, which usually generate greater thirst. It is very important to maintain proper electrolyte balance by eating small quantities of nutritional foods throughout the day, even if you feel you don't have an appetite.

Changeable Weather

The desert is well known for sudden changes in the weather. The temperature can change 50 degrees in less than an hour. Prepare yourself with extra food and clothing, rain/wind gear, and a flashlight. When leaving on a trip, let someone know your exact route, especially if traveling solo, and your estimated time of return; don't forget to let them know when you get back. Register your route at the closest park office or backcountry board, especially for longer hikes that involve cross-country travel.

Hypothermia/Hyperthermia

Abrupt chilling is as much a danger in the desert as heat stroke. Storms and/or nightfall can cause desert temperatures to plunge. Wear layers of clothes, adding or subtracting depending on conditions, to avoid overheating or chilling. At the other extreme, you need to protect yourself from sun and wind with proper clothing. The broad-brimmed hat is mandatory equipment for the desert traveler. Even in the cool days of winter, a delightful time in the desert, the sun's rays are intense.

Vegetation

You quickly will learn not to come in contact with certain desert vegetation. Catclaw, Spanish bayonet, and cacti are just a few of the botanical hazards that will get your attention if you become complacent. Carry tweezers to extract cactus spines. Wear long pants if traveling off-trail or in a brushy area. Many folks carry a hair comb to assist with removal of cholla balls.

Rattlesnakes, Scorpions, Tarantulas

These desert "creepy crawlies" are easily terrified by unexpected human visitors, and they react predictably to being frightened. Do not sit or put your hands in dark places you can't see, especially during the warmer "snake season" months. Carry and know how to use your snakebite-venom-extractor kit for emergencies when help is far away. In the event of a snakebite, seek medical assistance as quickly as possible. Keep tents zipped and always shake out boots, packs, and clothes before putting them on.

Mountain Lions

The California desert is mountain-lion country. Avoid hiking at night, when lions are often hunting. Instruct your children on appropriate behavior when confronted with a lion. Do not run. Keep children in sight while hiking; stay close to them in areas where lions might hide.

Mine Hazards

The California desert contains thousands of deserted mines. All of them should be considered hazardous. Stay away from all mines and mine structures. The vast majority of these mines have not been secured or even posted. Keep an eye on young or adventuresome members of your group.

Hanta Virus

In addition to the mines, there are often deserted buildings around the mine sites. Hanta virus is a deadly disease carried by deer mice in the Southwest. Any enclosed area increases the chances of breathing the airborne particles that carry this life-threatening virus. As a precaution, do not enter deserted buildings.

Flash Floods

Desert washes and canyons can become traps for unwary visitors when rainstorms hit the desert. Keep a watchful eye on the sky. Never camp in flash-flood areas. Check at a ranger station on regional weather conditions before embarking on your back-country expedition. A storm anywhere upstream in a drainage can result in a sudden torrent in a lower canyon. Do not cross a flooded wash. Both the depth and the current can be deceiving; wait for the flood to recede, which usually does not take long.

Lightning

Be aware of lightning, especially during summer storms. Stay off ridges and peaks. Shallow overhangs and gullies should also be avoided because electrical current often moves at ground level near a lightning strike.

Unstable Rocky Slopes

Desert canyons and mountainsides often consist of crumbly or fragmented rock. Mountain sheep are better adapted to this terrain than us bipeds. Use caution when climbing; the downward journey is usually the more hazardous. Smooth rock faces such as in slickrock canyons are equally dangerous, especially when you've got sand on the soles of your boots. On those rare occasions when they are wet, the rocks are slicker than ice.

Giardia

Any surface water, with the possible exception of springs where they flow out of the ground, is apt to contain *Giardia lamblia*, a microorganism that causes severe diarrhea. Boil water for at least five minutes or use a filter system. Iodine drops are not effective in killing this pesky parasite.

Zero-Impact Desert Etiquette

The desert environment is fragile; damage lasts for decades—even centuries. Desert courtesy requires us to leave no evidence that we were ever there. This ethic means no grafitti or defoliation at one end of the spectrum, and no unnecessary footprints on delicate vegetation on the other. Here are seven general guidelines for desert wilderness behavior:

Avoid making new trails. If hiking cross-country, stay on one set of footprints when traveling in a group. Try to make your route invisible. Desert vegetation grows very slowly. Its destruction leads to wind and water erosion and irreparable harm to the desert. Darker crusty soil that crumbles easily indicates cryptogamic soils, which are a living blend of tightly bonded mosses, lichens, and bacteria. This dark crust prevents wind and water erosion and protects seeds that fall into the soil. Walking can destroy this fragile layer. Take special care to avoid stepping on cryptogamic soil.

Keep noise down. Desert wilderness means quiet and solitude, for the animal life as well as other human visitors.

Leave your pets at home. Check with park authorities before including your dog in the group. Share other experiences with your best friend, not the desert.

Pack it in/pack it out. This is more true in the desert than anywhere else. Desert winds spread debris, and desert air preserves it. Always carry a trash bag, both for your trash and for any that you encounter. If you must smoke, pick up your butts and bag them. Bag and carry out toilet paper (it doesn't deteriorate in the desert) and feminine hygiene products.

Never camp near water. Most desert animals are nocturnal, and most, like the bighorn sheep, are exceptionally shy. The presence of humans is very disturbing, so camping near their water source means they will go without water. Camp in already-used sites if possible to reduce further damage. If none is available, camp on ground that is already bare. And use a camp stove. Ground fires are forbidden in most desert parks; gathering wood is also not permitted. Leave your campsite as you found it. Better yet, improve it by picking up litter, cleaning out fire rings, or scattering ashes of any inconsiderate predecessors. Remember that artifacts fifty years old or older are protected by federal law and must not be moved or removed.

Treat human waste properly. Bury human waste 4 inches deep and at least 200 feet from water and trails. Pack out toilet paper and feminine hygiene products; they do not decompose in the arid desert. Do not burn toilet paper; many wildfires have been started this way.

Respect wildlife. Living in the desert is hard enough without being harassed by human intruders. Remember this is the only home these animals have. They treasure their privacy. Be respectful and use binoculars for long-distance viewing. Especially important: Do not molest the rare desert water sources by playing or bathing in them.

Beyond these guidelines, refer to the park's regulations for specific rules governing backcountry usage. Enjoy the beauty and solitude of the desert, and leave it for others to enjoy.

How to Use This Book

This guide is the source book for those who wish to experience on foot the very best hikes and backcountry trips the vast and varied Joshua Tree desert has to offer. Hikers are given many choices from which they can pick and choose, depending on their wishes and abilities.

The maps in this book that depict a detailed close-up of an area use elevation tints, called hypsometry, to portray relief. Each gray tone represents a range of equal elevation, as shown in the scale key with the map. These maps will give you a good idea of elevation gain and loss. The darker tones are lower elevations and the lighter grays are higher elevations. The lighter the tone, the higher the elevation. Narrow bands of different gray tones spaced closely together indicate steep terrain, whereas wider bands indicate areas of more gradual slope.

Maps that show larger geographic areas use shaded, or shadow, relief. Shadow relief does not represent elevation; it demonstrates slope or relative steepness. This gives an almost 3-D perspective of the physiography of a region and will help you see where ranges and valleys are.

Begin by referring to the hike locator map on page 12, along with the "Hikes at a Glance" matrix, for a quick overview of all of the hikes presented for the park. After making your selections, turn to the specific hike descriptions for added detail. Each hike is numbered and named and begins with a general description. This overview briefly describes the type of hike and highlights the destination and key features.

The "start" is the approximate road distance from a nearby town or park visitor center to the trailhead. The idea is to give you a mental picture of where the hike is in relation to your prospective travels.

Hike "distance" is given in total miles for the described route. The mileage is in one direction for a loop, in which you return to the place where you started without retracing your steps, or for a one-way hike, in which you begin at one trailhead and end at another, requiring two vehicles, a shuttle bus, or another driver to pick you up or deposit you at either end. Round-trip mileage is provided for an out-and-back hike, in which you return to the trailhead the same way you came. A lollipop loop combines a stretch of out-and-back with a loop at one end. Mileages were calculated in the field and double-checked as accurately as possible with the most detailed topographic maps.

"Approximate hiking time" provides a best guess as to how long it will take the average hiker to complete the route. Always add more time for further exploration or for contemplation.

The "difficulty" rating is necessarily subjective, but it is based on the authors' extensive backcountry experience with folks of all ages and abilities. Easy hikes present no difficulty to hikers of all abilities. Moderate hikes are challenging to inexperienced hikers and might tax even experienced hikers. Strenuous hikes are extremely difficult and challenging, even for the most-seasoned hikers. Distance, elevation gain and loss, trail condition, and terrain were considered in assigning the difficulty rating. There are, of course, many variables. The easiest hike can be sheer torture if you run out of water in extreme heat—a definite no-no.

"Trail surfaces" are evaluated based on well-defined trail standards. Dirt trails have no obstructions and are easy to follow. Rocky trails may be partially blocked by slides, rocks, or debris but are generally obvious and easy to find. Primitive trails are faint, rough, and rocky and may have disappeared completely in places. In the desert some of the best hiking takes place on old four-wheel-drive mining roads that are now closed to vehicular use because of wilderness designation or to protect key values, such as wildlife watering holes. Many of the desert hikes are off-trail in washes, canyons, ridges, and fans. "Use trails" may form a segment of the route. A use trail is simply an informal, unconstructed path created solely by the passage of hikers.

The best "season" is based largely on the moderate-temperature months for the particular hike and is greatly influenced by elevation. Additional consideration is given to seasonal road access at higher altitudes. The range of months given is not necessarily the best time for wildflowers, which is highly localized and dependent on elevation and rainfall. Nor is it necessarily the best time to view wildlife, which may be during the driest and hottest summer months near water sources.

Two maps are listed for each hike—the National Geographic Trails Illustrated Joshua Tree National Park (map 226), and the US Geological Survey 7.5-minute topographic map(s). The Trails Illustrated map covers the entire park and is printed on waterproof paper. It has the most up-to-date road, campground, and trail information. The USGS topo maps are the most detailed maps available and are essential if you plan to hike off-trail, though the roads and trails shown are often out of date. See Appendix C for map sources.

For more information on the hike, the best available "trail contact" for the park management agency is listed. See appendix D for a complete listing of all agency addresses and phone numbers.

"Finding the trailhead" includes detailed up-to-date driving instructions to the trailhead or jumping-off point for each hike. Most hikes have a signed, formal trailhead, but a few only have an informal parking area. To follow these instructions, start with the beginning reference point, which might be the park visitor center, a nearby town, or an important road junction. Pay close attention to mileage and landmark instructions. American Automobile Association (AAA) map mileages are used when available, but in many instances we had to rely on our car odometer, which may vary slightly from other car odometers. To help you find the traihead, the GPS coordinates are listed for each trailhead, in latitude/longitude format.

The text following the driving directions is a narrative of the actual route, with general directions and key features noted. In some cases interpretation of the natural and cultural history of the hike and its surroundings is included. The idea is to provide accurate route-finding instructions, with enough supporting information to enhance your enjoyment of the hike without diminishing your sense of discovery—a fine line indeed. Some of these descriptions are augmented with photographs that preview a representative segment of the hike.

The trail itinerary, "Miles and Directions," provides detailed mile-by-mile instructions while noting landmarks, trail junctions, canyon entrances, dry falls, peaks, and historic sites along the way.

And last, please don't allow our value-laden list of "favorite hikes" (appendix A) to discourage you from completing any of the other hikes. They're all worth doing!

Joshua Tree National Park

Joshua Tree National Park Overview

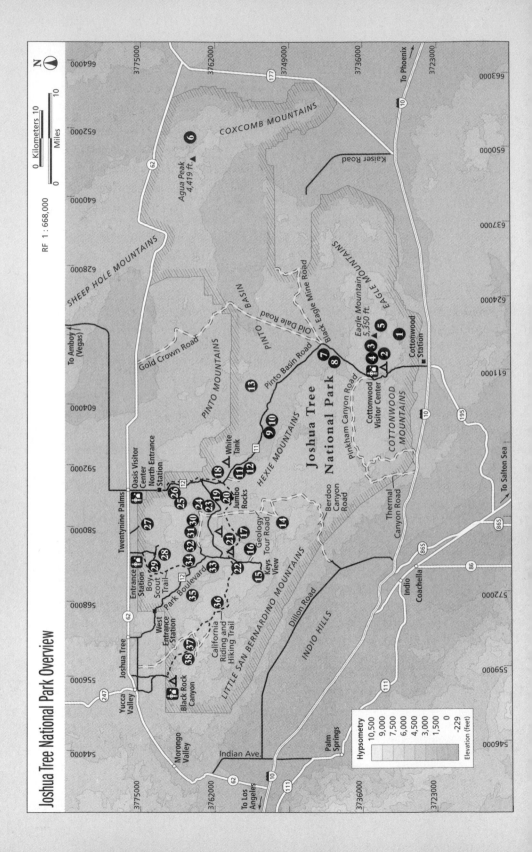

1 Lost Palms Oasis

Right at the southern edge of the park is an oasis with the largest group of California fan palms in Joshua Tree National Park. Take this moderate out-and-back hike to an overlook, then continue down to the oasis, and go even farther down Lost Palms Canyon if you're up for it.

Start: 42 miles southeast of Twentynine Palms and 1.2 miles southeast of Cottonwood Visitor Center.
Distance: 7.6 miles out and back.
Approximate hiking time: 4 to 6 hours.
Difficulty: Moderate.

Trail surface: Dirt path.
Seasons: October through April.
Maps: Trails Illustrated Joshua Tree National Park; USGS Cottonwood Spring.
Trail contact: Joshua Tree National Park (see appendix D).

Finding the trailhead: From California Highway 62 in Twentynine Palms, take Utah Trail south 4 miles to the North Entrance of the park; continue south on Park Route 12 4.8 miles to the Pinto Y intersection. Turn left onto Park Route 11 and go 32 miles to the Cottonwood Visitor Center. Turn left and drive 1.2 miles to the Cottonwood Spring parking area. GPS: N33 44.21400' / W115 48.6438'

From the south, take the Cottonwood Canyon exit from Interstate 10, 24 miles east of Indio. Go north 8 miles to the Cottonwood Visitor Center. Turn right and go 1.2 miles to the Cottonwood Spring parking area.

The Hike

This is a dry, high hike with no protection from sun and wind. It is a heavily signed route, with arrows at every bend and every wash crossing, and even mileage posts.

The trail follows the up-and-down topography of the ridge-and-wash terrain. At each ridge, one hopes to spot the oasis ahead, particularly if it is a hot and sunny day. Not until the final overlook will such hopes be realized. And after crossing numerous ridges, descending rocky paths to narrow canyons, and winding up to more ridges, it is a welcome site!

This is the largest group of California fan palms in Joshua Tree National Park, and they are majestic. The oasis is a day-use-only area to protect bighorn-sheep access to water; you may be lucky enough to spot one of the elusive animals on the rocky slopes above the oasis.

A rocky path leads 0.3 mile from the overlook to the oasis. Large boulders, intermittent streams, willow thickets, and sandy beaches make this a delightful spot in which to pause before your return trip.

Miles and Directions

0.0 The trail begins above the oasis at Cottonwood Spring. The well-marked trail goes up a wash and over a ridge. Continue straight to the oasis.

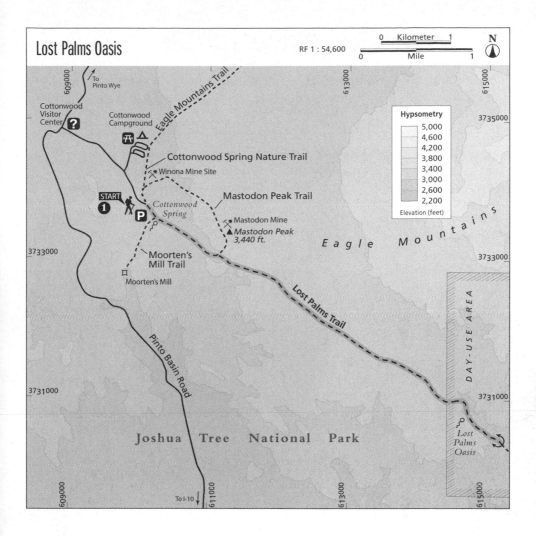

Lost Palms Oasis

RF 1 : 54,600

Hypsometry

Elevation (feet)
5,000
4,600
4,200
3,800
3,400
3,000
2,600
2,200

To Pinto Wye

Cottonwood Visitor Center

Cottonwood Campground

Eagle Mountains Trail

Cottonwood Spring Nature Trail

Winona Mine Site

Mastodon Peak Trail

START
1

Cottonwood Spring

Mastodon Mine

Mastodon Peak
3,440 ft.

Eagle   Mountains

Moorten's Mill Trail

Moorten's Mill

Lost Palms Trail

Pinto Basin Road

DAY-USE AREA

Joshua   Tree   National   Park

Lost Palms Oasis

To I-10

3.5 View the palm oasis from the canyon overlook.

3.8 Reach the floor of the oasis.

7.6 Return to the trailhead.

Option: The more energetic hiker may like to continue about another mile down the canyon through the willows and around the pools, along an intermittent rusty pipe that was used to channel water to a mining site far to the south. The trail, such as it is, becomes more challenging, with larger boulders to contend with, but at the end you'll reach another set of palm trees—the Victory Palms. When your rock-scrambling is satisfied, it is time to return to the oasis, and retrace your steps to the spring.

◀   *Looking south from Lost Palms Oasis toward Victory Palms and Chiriaco Summit.*

2 Cottonwood Spring/Moorten's Mill Site

A short hike down Cottonwood Wash allows you to enjoy a lush spring, an arid desert wash, and a historic mining site—truly a cross section of the variety of Joshua Tree National Park.

Start: 42 miles southeast of Twentynine Palms and 1.2 miles southeast of Cottonwood Visitor Center.
Distance: 1 mile out and back.
Approximate hiking time: Less than 1 hour.
Difficulty: Easy.

Trail surface: Sandy wash.
Seasons: October through April.
Maps: Trails Illustrated Joshua Tree National Park; USGS Cottonwood Spring.
Trail contact: Joshua Tree National Park (see appendix D).

The road ramp at Little Chilcoot Pass, built by miners in the 1800s, enabled freight wagons to bypass the rock waterfall in Cottonwood Canyon.

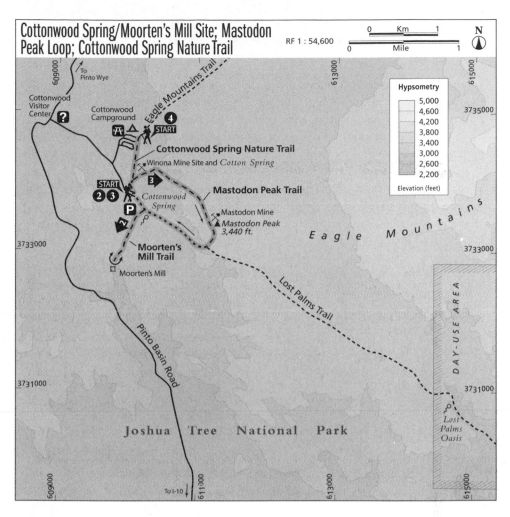

Cottonwood Spring/Moorten's Mill Site; Mastodon Peak Loop; Cottonwood Spring Nature Trail

RF 1 : 54,600

Hypsometry

5,000
4,600
4,200
3,800
3,400
3,000
2,600
2,200

Elevation (feet)

To Pinto Wye

Cottonwood Visitor Center

Cottonwood Campground

Eagle Mountains Trail

START **4**

Cottonwood Spring Nature Trail

Winona Mine Site and *Cotton Spring*

START **2 3**

3

Cottonwood Spring

Mastodon Peak Trail

Mastodon Mine
Mastodon Peak
3,440 ft.

Eagle Mountains

Moorten's Mill Trail

Moorten's Mill

Lost Palms Trail

DAY-USE AREA

Pinto Basin Road

Joshua Tree National Park

Lost Palms Oasis

To I-10

3735000

3733000

3733000

3731000

3731000

Finding the trailhead: From Twentynine Palms, take Utah Trail south 4 miles from California Highway 62 to the North Entrance of the park. Continue south on Park Route 12 for 4.8 miles to the left turn on Park Route 11 at the Pinto Y intersection (signed for Cottonwood Spring). Drive south 32 miles to the Cottonwood Campground and Visitor Center. Turn left and drive 1.2 miles to the parking area. The oasis is down the ramp to the southeast; you can see the palm trees from the parking lot. GPS: N33 44.21400' / W115 48.6438'

From the south, take Interstate 10 24 miles east of Indio to the Cottonwood Canyon exit; turn north and continue 8 miles to the Cottonwood Campground and Visitor Center. Turn right and drive 1.2 miles to the parking area.

The Hike

Cottonwood Spring is a lovely patch of greenery in an otherwise arid landscape. The cottonwoods are natives. The palms appeared around 1920, probably by seeds transported by the birds. The sight is satisfying, and obviously the birds enjoy the location.

The hike down the wash provides a display of a wash plant community in the Colorado Desert. Mesquite and smoke trees are dominant.

The ramp around the boulders in the wash will be quite a surprise. The determination of the miners of the last century to use this route for their vehicles is noteworthy. The ramp is massive; yet even with it in place, the trek up or down the wash must have been arduous with a loaded wagon.

Seeing the mill site will cure any thought of romanticizing the life of the prospector in these parts. Although the wash is lovely for its solitude and silence, living here must have been grim. "Cactus" Slim Moorten was here for less than ten years. All that remains of his mill are pieces of rusty equipment and rusting car parts.

The hike back up the wash brings you back to the oasis, which looks greener than ever after a sojourn into drier country.

Miles and Directions

0.0 From the parking lot, take the ramp down to the oasis.

0.1 After enjoying the spring area, continue south in the wash.

0.25 Boulders block the easy wash; to the right is a section of road constructed by miners in the 1880s. This is Little Chilcoot Pass.

0.5 Moorten's Mill Site is the turnaround point. There's a trailpost in the center of the wash.

1.0 Return to the trailhead.

3 Mastodon Peak Loop

A loop hike, the Mastodon route winds by a historic mining site and takes you to the top of the monzogranite mound that resembles a prehistoric elephant for those with an imagination. On the return leg, you can enjoy the greenery at Cottonwood Spring.

See map on page 17.
Start: 42 miles southeast of Twentynine Palms and 1.2 miles southeast of Cottonwood Visitor Center.
Distance: 3-mile loop.
Approximate hiking time: 1.5 to 3 hours.
Difficulty: Easy; moderate if the peak is included. The peak requires some scrambling but provides excellent views.

Trail surface: Dirt path.
Seasons: October through April.
Maps: Trails Illustrated Joshua Tree National Park; USGS Cottonwood Spring.
Trail contact: Joshua Tree National Park (see appendix D).

Finding the trailhead: From California Highway 62 in Twentynine Palms, take Utah Trail south 4 miles to the North Entrance of the park; continue on Park Route 12 for 4.8 miles to the Pinto

From this vantage point—and if you squint—the mound of granite does resemble a mastodon.

Y intersection. Turn left onto Park Route 11 and go south 32 miles to Cottonwood Visitor Center. Turn left and go 1.2 miles to the oasis.

From the south, take the Cottonwood Canyon exit from Interstate 10, 24 miles east of Indio; go north 8 miles to Cottonwood Visitor Center, then right (east) 1.2 miles to the Cottonwood Spring parking lot. GPS: N33 44.21400' / W115 48.6438'

Walk west from the parking lot, back up the road 0.1 mile to beginning of the nature trail on your right. Walk up the nature trail 0.3 mile to the junction with the Mastodon Peak route. From the Cottonwood Campground, the trail begins 0.2 mile from campsite no. 13A on loop A, via the nature trail segment, which begins at the campground and meets at the same junction.

The Hike

This trail takes you by two historic sites and a lofty overlook of the southern region of the park. Either approach to the trail includes the nature trail. The view of the old gold mill and the mine is in direct contrast with the Indians' use of the riches of the desert; the latter left no ruins or scars on the environment.

The trail is clearly marked with signposts and a rock-lined path. The lower section of the hike is up a sandy wash to the Winona mill site. Building foundations and other remnants are all that remain of the mill that refined the gold from the Mastodon mine in the 1920s. The exotic plant specimens at adjacent Cotton Spring were planted by the Hulsey family, who owned the mill and mine.

The trail winds up the hill above the mill to the mine, which was operated by George Hulsey between 1919 and 1932, when it was abandoned. Carefully thread your way up by the sign above the mine and through the mine ruins (in direct contradiction of park warnings to stay clear of old mines) to a trailpost and arrow pointing east. A major freeway–style sign indicates your options and the various distances to the spring, the oasis, and the peak from this point.

The climb to the peak (0.1 mile) is on an unsigned trail, although the well–used path is easy to discern, and cairns appear at critical spots. The use trail goes to the right of a boulder pile, across a slab of granite, and winds around to the northeast side of the peak to the summit, on the opposite side from the mine site. Minor boulder scrambling is necessary. The view is well worth the effort.

After the peak the trail resumes its zigzag rocky path through the canyon, well signed with arrows. It is on this portion of the trail that you can see clearly the elephant likeness in the peak behind you. About 0.4 mile after the peak is the intersection with the Lost Palms Trail. Turn right for the walk down the winding trail to Cottonwood Spring and the parking lot. Turn left for the longer hike to Lost Palms Oasis (6.3 miles round–trip from this junction and back to the parking lot).

Miles and Directions

0.0–0.2 Take the nature trail from the parking area.

0.5 At the junction with Mastodon Peak Trail, turn right and immediately encounter the Winona mill ruins and Cotton Spring.

1.5 The trail continues above the Mastodon Mine.

1.6 At this junction, turn left to the peak (0.1 mile round-trip).

2.0 At the junction with the Lost Palms Trail, turn right to return to the parking area.

2.6 At Cottonwood Spring, continue up the ramp to the parking area.

3.0 Return to the trailhead.

4 Cottonwood Spring Nature Trail

This easy out-and-back nature trail identifies the desert plants and provides information about their use by Native Americans.

See map on page 17.
Start: 42 miles southeast of Twentynine Palms and 1.2 miles southeast of the Cottonwood Visitor Center.
Distance: 1.2 miles out and back.
Approximate hiking time: 1 hour or less.
Difficulty: Easy.

Trail surface: Dirt path.
Seasons: October through April.
Maps: Trails Illustrated Joshua Tree National Park; USGS Cottonwood Spring.
Trail contact: Joshua Tree National Park (see appendix D).

Finding the trailhead: From California Highway 62 in Twentynine Palms, take Utah Trail south 4 miles to the North Entrance; continue south on Park Route 12 for 4.8 miles to the Pinto Y intersection. Turn left onto Park Route 11 and go 32 miles to Cottonwood Visitor Center. Turn left and go 1.2 miles to the Cottonwood Spring parking area. GPS: N33 44.21400' / W115 48.6438'

Walk 0.1 mile west along the road to the nature trail on your right. The trail also begins at the eastern ends of loops A and B in the campground and goes to Cottonwood Spring. If you're not camping there, however, it is not possible to park at the campground.

From the south, take the Cottonwood Canyon exit from Interstate 10, 24 miles east of Indio, and drive north 8 miles to the Cottonwood Visitor Center. Turn right and go 1.2 miles to the parking area.

The Hike

The broad clear trail leads up a wash from the road near the spring, eventually winding up to a low ridge leading to the campground. This is one of the most informative nature trails in the park. The signs are legible, placed with the appropriate plants, and highly educational.

The information on this nature trail identifies the plants common to this region of the Colorado (Sonoran) Desert. The unique focus of the signs is on the Cahuilla Indians' use of the plants for food, medicine, and household goods. A Cahuilla elder provided the information. The detailed explanations of the processes used by the original inhabitants create genuine admiration for their sophistication. Several of the plants originally developed by the Indians are now grown and marketed commercially, such as creosote tea and jojoba.

If you choose to continue on to the Mastodon Peak Trail, that intersection is halfway down the nature trail from its northern end. Or you can walk back down to the parking lot, reviewing the new information you have learned.

5 Conejo Well/Eagle Mountains

A long but gently graded walk across the open Colorado Desert takes you through a gap in the remote Eagle Mountains to the remains of a historic well site. This is a long outing, suitable only for those with skills in cross-country navigation.

Start: 42 miles southeast of Twentynine Palms and 1.2 miles southeast of Cottonwood Visitor Center.
Distance: 12 miles out and back.
Approximate hiking time: 5 to 7 hours.
Difficulty: Moderate.
Trail surface: Dirt path, sandy wash.

Seasons: October through April.
Maps: Trails Illustrated Joshua Tree National Park; USGS Porcupine Wash-CA; Conejo Well-CA; and Cottonwood Spring.
Trail contact: Joshua Tree National Park (see appendix D).

Looking northeast from the Eagle Mountain Trail at mile 2.

Finding the trailhead: From California Highway 62 in Twentynine Palms, take Utah Trail south 4 miles to the park's North Entrance; continue south on Park Route 12 for 4.8 miles to the Pinto Y intersection. Bear left onto Park Route 11 and drive 32 miles south to Cottonwood Visitor Center. Turn left and go 1.2 miles to the campground. The trail begins at campsite no. 17 on the B loop.

From the south, take the Cottonwood Canyon exit north from Interstate 10, 24 miles east of Indio; go north 8 miles to Cottonwood Visitor Center. Turn right and go 1.2 miles to the Cottonwood Spring parking area. GPS: N33 44.21400' / W115 48.6438'

The Hike

The clear, well-defined trail is actually a closed four-wheel-drive mining road. It takes off in a northeasterly direction from the Cottonwood Campground. The first 100 yards pass a series of planted shrubs. The Eagle Mountains rise to the southeast above an alluvial fan coated with cholla, creosote, and yucca. The trail continues up a sandy wash marked every so often by rock cairns. At 0.5 mile the wash splits; stay left. The old two-track is plainly visible for the most part, continuing in a nearly straight line.

At 2 miles the trail cuts north and crosses a large rock-walled wash. For the next 0.5 mile, it crosses several side washes and small ridges. At this point it is heading northeast toward a broad sloping pass through the north end of the Eagle Mountains. For a strenuous side climb to 5,350-foot Eagle Peak, leave the trail at around mile 3 for a good approach. Look for a broad ridge leading to the south for a route to this apex of the Eagle Mountain Range.

At mile 3 California juniper become more prevalent along with denser clumps of yucca. The trail tops the broad pass at 3,440 feet then follows a wide wash through a gap in the Eagle Mountains, with Eagle Peak rising ruggedly to the south. The

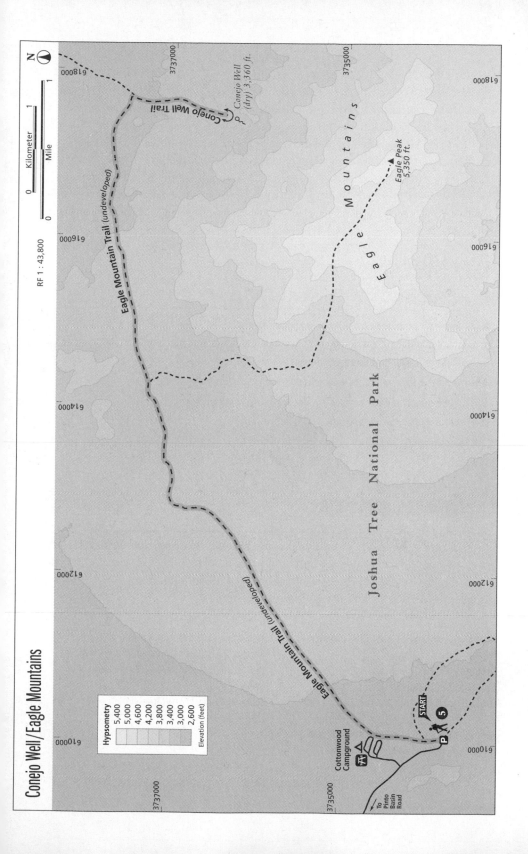

Conejo Well/Eagle Mountains

RF 1 : 43,800

Hypsometry
5,400
5,000
4,600
4,200
3,800
3,400
3,000
2,600
Elevation (feet)

Cottonwood Campground

To Pinto Basin Road

START
P 5

Eagle Mountain Trail (undeveloped)

Eagle Mountain Trail (undeveloped)

Conejo Well Trail

Conejo Well (dry) 3,360 ft.

Eagle Mountains

Eagle Peak 5,350 ft.

Joshua Tree National Park

N

0 1 Kilometer
0 1 Mile

junction to the Conejo Well site takes off to the right (south) at 5.3 miles in a garden of cholla. This junction is easy to miss, but it is marked by a rock cairn.

The Conejo Well trail takes off at a 45-degree angle to the right up the left side of a swale in a patch of brittlebush. It heads south toward a rugged canyon on the north side of Eagle Mountain. After another 0.5 mile, it enters the mouth of a narrow rocky canyon distinguished by columns of red rock jutting upward to the slopes of Eagle Mountain. The old mining road climbs another 0.2 mile to the well site, where only a few rusted pipes and cans are found. Depending on the light, a shallow cave appears to overlook the well site 0.3 mile upslope. In fact, the dark opening is merely a shallow rock overhang. Retrace your route to complete this 12-mile round-trip exploration of remote Colorado Desert country.

This hike is considered a cross-country route of travel by the park. It should be undertaken only by hikers with navigation skills.

Miles and Directions

0.0 The path gradually climbs from the trailhead.

3.0 The trail begins a gentle ascent to the high point of 3,440 feet. A possible cross-country route to Eagle Peak leads to the south.

4.5 The trail crosses a prominent northeast-southwest trending wash.

5.3 At the junction with the trail to Conejo Well, turn right (south).

6.0 Arrive at the Conejo Well site.

12.0 Return to the trailhead.

6 Coxcomb Mountains

The Coxcombs lie in the wildest and most remote corner of the park. Here you can achieve a profound feeling of solitude, with hidden basins, expansive vistas, and jagged jumbles of granite in every direction. Not a hike for the novice, this outing requires advanced skills in cross-country navigation.

Start: About 45 miles east of Twentynine Palms.
Distance: 17 miles out and back.
Approximate hiking time: 6 to 8 hours.
Difficulty: Difficult for the suggested route; peak climbing in this region is strenuous.
Trail surface: Sandy washes with moderate bouldering at the mouth of the canyon.

Seasons: October through May.
Maps: Trails Illustrated Joshua Tree National Park; USGS Cadiz Valley SW-CA and Cadiz Valley SE.
Trail contact: Joshua Tree National Park (see appendix D).

Looking down the bouldery Coxcomb Canyon at mile 0.3. ▶

Finding the trailhead: From Twentynine Palms, at the traffic light junction of Twentynine Palms and Adobe Road, drive east on California Highway 62 (Twentynine Palms Highway) 41.9 miles to an unsigned sandy dirt road, which is also 1.9 miles east of a parking turnout. This is a difficult road to find, so watch carefully. GPS: N34°05.71020' / W115°25.22880'

The Hike

The Coxcombs are likely the most rugged and perpendicular mountains in Joshua Tree National Park, in its wildest and least-visited northeast corner. Their relative isolation alone, far from any services, makes their exploration a true wilderness experience. The recommended starting point for this hike provides the easiest access into the Coxcombs. It is also the only access from the north; the southern access point is at Pinto Wells.

From the parking area at the highway, follow an old road 4.5 miles aouth and southeast to the mouth of the canyon northwest of of Aqua Peak.

The mouth of the canyon is blocked by huge boulders, a somewhat formidable beginning to this otherwise moderate hike. Begin by taking a use trail to the right up and around the first set of boulders. The remaining boulders are easy to scramble over and around for the next 0.25 mile to where the sandy wash opens up and provides easy walking. The open wash also provides magnificent views of the rugged Coxcombs, especially to the right (south-southwest), with their great slanting blocks and vertical columns of reddish rock.

At 0.5 mile the wash splits; stay to the left and continue southeast up the smaller of the two washes. At 0.8 mile the first low pass is reached. Continue to the southeast on a faint use trail, which drops down a series of small ridges and gullies toward the large wash seen far in the distance. Cathedral-like rock spires tower overhead. At 1 mile the confines of a rocky wash are reached. At 1.4 miles the wash widens, joined by another wash from the right, with spectacular vistas back to the northwest. Continue down another 0.3 mile to where the main wash turns sharply to the left (north). This canyon wash is worth exploring as a side trip if time permits. It leads north to northeast another 1.5 miles to a canyon entrance that opens to a broad alluvial fan on the north side of the mountains.

Return to the junction at mile 1.7. The side wash entering from the left (southeast) is the route to the Inner Valley. Hike southeasterly up this winding but widening wash. At 2.1 miles a wash enters from the right; continue to the left up the main wash. Soon the country opens up into the lower end of the Inner Valley—a vast plateaulike expanse of open desert ringed by jagged spires, mounds, and formations of rocks—white to red and in every conceivable shape. The wash bends around to the right and heads southwest up the broad alluvial fan of the upper reaches of the valley. The fan/wash rises gradually for another mile to a prominent pass at mile 3.5 (3,090 feet), which serves as a panoramic overlook of the vast desert of Pinto Basin to the south. Hold on to your hat: This is also a natural wind tunnel.

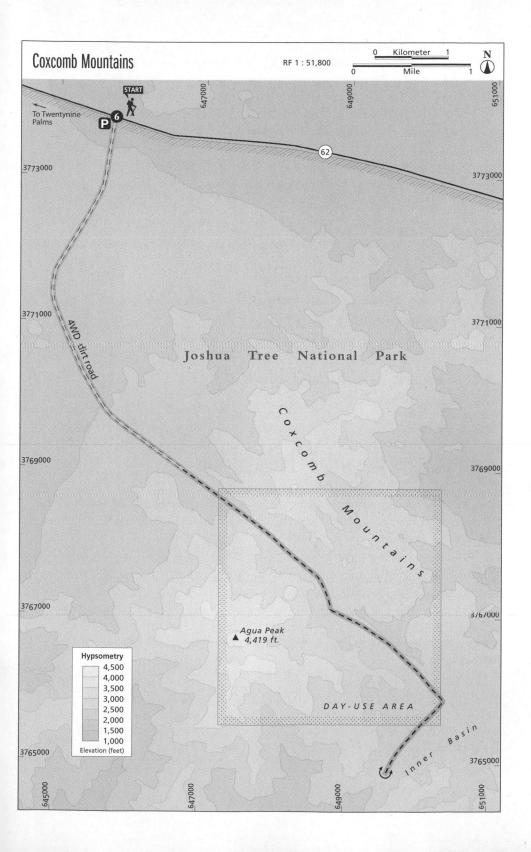

Coxcomb Mountains

RF 1 : 51,800

Kilometer

Mile

N

To Twentynine Palms

START

P 6

62

Joshua Tree National Park

4WD dirt road

Coxcomb Mountains

DAY-USE AREA

Inner Basin

Agua Peak
▲ 4,419 ft.

Hypsometry

4,500
4,000
3,500
3,000
2,500
2,000
1,500
1,000

Elevation (feet)

3773000
3771000
3769000
3767000
3765000

645000
647000
649000
651000

Retrace your route to complete this 17-mile round-trip. If you're planning to stay overnight, find a sheltered campsite in the upper valley near the overlook or in the lower east end of the valley outside the day-use area that includes much of this route—the limit is meant to protect wildlife, including rare desert bighorns. There are many tantalizing opportunities for boulder scrambling and canyoneering on all sides of the Inner Valley, particularly into some of the larger side canyons bordering the east side of the valley near the overlook. Overnight backpackers would need to carry at least two gallons of water per person per day.

This hike should be undertaken only by hikers skilled in cross-country navigation.

Miles and Directions

0.0 Parking area on Highway 62.

5.0 Reach the mouth of the canyon (2,640 feet).

5.3 You have to scramble over some boulders before arriving at a sandy wash.

5.8 Arrive at a low pass (2,970 feet).

6.7 A side wash enters from the southeast; continue up this wash.

7.5 Arrive at the Inner Valley.

8.5 Arrive at the Pinto Basin Overlook (3,090 feet).

17.0 Return to the trailhead.

7 Porcupine Wash/Ruby Lee Mill Site

This is a loop hike, requiring competence in cross-country navigation because it is not on a park-maintained trail. You have the opportunity of finding a historic mining site as well as petroglyphs on the route.

Start: About 30 miles southeast of Twentynine Palms and 8 miles north of Cottonwood Visitor Center.
Distance: 7.9-mile loop.
Approximate hiking time: 4 to 5 hours.
Difficulty: Moderate.

Trail surface: Dirt path, sandy wash.
Seasons: October through April.
Maps: Trails Illustrated Joshua Tree National Park; USGS Porcupine Wash.
Trail contact: Joshua Tree National Park (see appendix D).

Finding the trailhead: From California Highway 62 in Twentynine Palms, take Utah Trail south 4 miles to the North Entrance; continue on Park Route 12 for 4.8 miles to the Pinto Y intersection. Bear left onto Park Route 11 and go 21.3 miles south to the Porcupine Wash Backcountry Board, on your right. GPS: N33°50.92260' / W115°46.83960'

Petroglyphs on granite boulder in Porcupine Wash.

From the south, take the Cottonwood Canyon exit from Interstate 10, 24 miles east of Indio. Go north 8 miles to the Cottonwood Entrance. Continue north 8.9 miles to the Porcupine Wash Backcountry Board, on your left.

The Hike

With topo map in hand, you will enjoy this moderate hike. Although the directions make it sound extremely complex, this is a very straightforward hike. The trail is fairly visible; moreover, the ridge to the east and the Hexie Mountains to the south are permanent markers, so you won't lose your bearings. The granite formations here are imaginative. Porcupine Wash is especially artistic with its smoke trees and water-sculpted boulders. The small S-curve canyon midway down the wash displays the power of water in this arid environment.

The variety of desert topography and vegetation is especially striking. The boulder-strewn sloping alluvial fan on the first half of the hike displays the vegetation typical of the Colorado Desert. Cholla cactus and creosote dominate the landscape. Curving through the foothills of the Hexie Range and dropping to the wash, you enter a new habitat—an active wash. The scouring action of flash flooding promotes the growth of smoke trees. The seeds require the grinding sands of floods to remove their protective covering in order to germinate, so instead of finding a water-swept wasteland, you find a smoke-tree paradise in the wash.

Porcupine Wash/Ruby Lee Mill Site; Porcupine Wash to Monument Mountain

RF 1 : 38,300

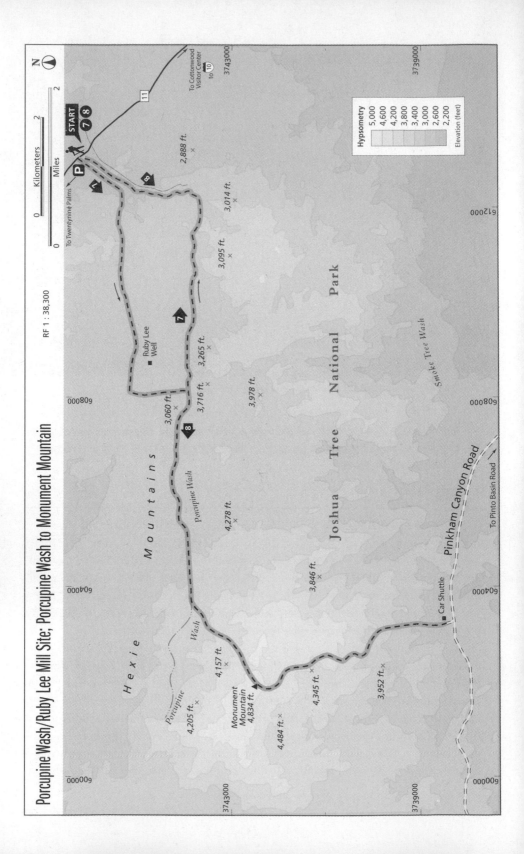

Porcupine Wash demonstrates a variety of wash architecture. Broad and narrow areas both exist, depending on the resistance of rock walls along the sides. The wash is wide at the junction with the Ruby Lee trail, but 2 miles farther east it becomes a slot canyon with narrow S-curves between the 200-foot-high walls. This narrow section lasts almost 0.5 mile before the wash opens again.

The mill site dates from the mid-1930s. The mill's career must have been quite brief, judging from its size. Not much is left. This area of Joshua Tree was not productive for mining.

A petroglyph site is located near the mouth of the wash. The rock face upon which the signs are engraved is turned to the east. Clearly these messages are intended for travelers approaching the entrance of the wash, en route toward Monument Mountain, visible directly to the west. Their meaning, however, remains a mystery. As is the case with all archaeological and historic artifacts, these are protected by federal law. Leave them untouched for others to enjoy.

Emerging from the wash, bear left along the foot of the ridge. By heading north you will shortly see the parking area and backcountry board to the northeast, guiding you back to your car.

This is not a maintained trail or route. It is quite washed out and invisible in places, and is considered cross-country travel by the park, for which hikers need a higher level of route-finding skills.

Miles and Directions

0.0–0.2 At the Porcupine Wash Backcountry Board, follow the jeep trail to the borrow pit southwest of the parking area.

0.2 Angle northwest across the alluvial fan. The trail heads toward a low notch at the far end of the ridge to the west.

1.5 At the broad high point (2,750 feet) marked with a cairn, the trail winds between granite boulders, with periodic cairns.

2.8 The wash narrows and the trail cuts between two boulder piles. Look for the small Ruby Lee Mill site, marked only with tailings, a stone foundation, the usual debris, and a small sign etched on a boulder.

3.0 The trail bears south. Cairns mark the route.

3.4 The trail drops to Porcupine Wash. Follow the wash left (east).

6.1 Beyond the canyon, bear left. Look for petroglyphs.

7.9 Return to the parking area.

8 Porcupine Wash to Monument Mountain

This outing is a strenuous point-to-point day hike to the highest peak in the Hexie Range, Monument Mountain (4,834 feet). You can savor sweeping views of the desert in every direction. It can also be done as an out-and-back hike to the peak.

See map on page 30.
Start: About 30 miles southeast of Twentynine Palms; 8 miles north of Cottonwood Visitor Center.
Distance: 14 miles one way (with car shuttle).
Approximate hiking time: 4 to 6 hours out and back to peak, or 6 to 7 hours for the shuttle hike.
Difficulty: Strenuous, with some moderately difficult boulder scrambling.

Trail surface: Clear wash use trail for 7.5 miles followed by 5.5 miles cross-country.
Seasons: October through April.
Maps: Trails Illustrated Joshua Tree National Park; USGS Porcupine Wash-CA and Washington Wash.
Trail contact: Joshua Tree National Park (see appendix D).

Finding the trailhead: From California Highway 62 in Twentynine Palms, take Utah Trail south 4 miles to the North Entrance; continue on Park Route 12 for 4.8 miles to the Pinto Y intersection. Bear left onto Park Route 11 and go 21.3 miles south to the Porcupine Wash Backcountry Board, on your right.

From the south, take the Cottonwood Canyon exit north from Interstate 10, 24 miles east of Indio. Go north 8 miles to the Cottonwood Visitor Center, then continue north 8.9 miles to the Porcupine Wash Backcountry Board, on your left. GPS: N33°50.92260' / W115°46.83960'

For a car shuttle: On Park Route 11, drive 8.9 miles south of the Porcupine Wash Backcountry Board to the Cottonwood Visitor Center. Turn right (north) on the four-wheel drive only Pinkham Canyon Road directly across the highway from the visitor center and drive 5.2 miles to the dirt road turnout on your right. Park here for the point-to-point pickup or the round-trip climb to Monument Mountain. GPS: N33°46.95000' / W115°52.57680'

The Hike

This hike requires skills in backcountry navigation. The route is not maintained by the park. From the backcountry board, head almost due south past the borrow pit, staying close to a line of boulders to your right. Within 0.5 mile Porcupine Wash becomes well defined. After about 1.5 miles the wash bends gradually to the right in a westerly direction. Another mile will bring you into a canyon with a series of S curves. The grade is gentle, and the open wash allows for easy going.

At 4.5 miles the remains of the old Ruby Lee Mill road come into view as it meets Porcupine Wash from the north (right). Continue up the wash through a low canyon and into a broad basin, distinguished by increasingly dense yucca. The wash itself is lined with creosote bushes and smoke trees. As the basin opens up, the distinctive cone summit of Monument Peak can be seen on the skyline to the southwest.

Jumbled rocks near the site of the Ruby Lee Mill.

Continue hiking up Porcupine Wash, passing a series of striking white rock columns at 5.2 miles. After another 0.1 mile the first large gully enters the main wash from the left. At 5.5 miles the remnants of the old overgrown four-wheel-drive road are visible on the right side of the canyon, but the wash offers easier walking. At 5.6 miles Monument Mountain can be seen to the southwest.

At 5.9 miles a second major side canyon enters from the left. Stay to the right on a bearing toward Monument Mountain. The valley widens here with an increasing density of yucca.

At 7 miles the peak drops below the ridge to the south. Continue up the wash another 0.5 mile before cutting cross-country southward toward the first line of high ridges. The country is open with scattered catclaw, creosote, and yucca. Up on the ridge at about 3,950 feet, the summit will present itself—as well as a suitable route around a series of deep canyons leading to the north ridge. This ridge requires more rock scrambling than other possible routes to the east, but the approach is more direct with fewer ups and downs. Upon reaching the summit, look for the peak register to learn of the experiences of previous climbers. More important, enjoy the spellbinding view with desert basins and ranges stretching as far as the eye can see.

To continue on a point-to-point route to Smoke Tree Wash on the Pinkham Canyon Road, take the southeast ridge for the shortest and easiest way down. The ridges and swales on the south side of the mountain are strewn with rugged outcrops of volcanic rock ribs that resemble backbones of dinosaurs. There is some up and down and a bit of route-finding on this serpentine ridge, but avoid the temptation to drop off of it for a "shortcut." This prominent southeast ridge offers the best and most enjoyable means of covering 3 miles and losing 1,600 feet to Smoke Tree Wash. After descending the foot of the ridge, hike about 1 mile across the flat to the road and your waiting shuttle vehicle. This point can also be the start and end of a cross-country climb (6 miles out and back) to Monument Mountain.

Miles and Directions

0.0–0.2 From the Porcupine Wash Backcountry Board, head south past the borrow pit.

0.2–1.5 Continue south up Porcupine Wash.

1.5–2.5 The wash trail winds up a series of S-curves in a canyon.

2.5–4.5 Continue up the wash.

4.5 The Ruby Lee jeep trail enters the wash from the right (north).

4.5–7.5 Continue up the wash into a broad basin.

7.5 Leave the wash for the cross-country route to the Monument summit.

10.0 Reach the summit of Monument Mountain.

14.0 Arrive at Pinkham Canyon Road (one-way hike).

Option: For an out-and-back trip, the route up to Monument Peak can be retraced back to the Porcupine Wash Backcountry Board, making for a long 20-mile day trip or a more reasonable overnight backpack with a night spent near Porcupine Wash if sufficient water is carried.

⑨ Golden Bee Mine

This is a fairly strenuous outing due to the rocky climb to the mine site. Once you get there you'll enjoy a magnificent view of the valley and surrounding mountain ranges.

Start: 18.6 miles south of Twentynine Palms.
Distance: 4.6 miles out and back.
Approximate hiking time: 2 to 4 hours.
Difficulty: Strenuous.
Trail surface: Dirt path, rocky wash, rocky trail.

Seasons: October through April.
Maps: Trails Illustrated Joshua Tree National Park; USGS Fried Liver Wash.
Trail contact: Joshua Tree National Park (see appendix D).

Finding the trailhead: From the park visitor center in Twentynine Palms, go south on Utah Trail 8.2 miles to the Pinto Y intersection. Bear left onto Park Route 11 and drive to the Cholla Cactus Garden Nature Trail. GPS: N33 55.532' / W115 55.728'

The lofty vantage point of the Golden Bee Mine provides a stunning vista of Pinto Basin.

The Hike

From the Cholla Cactus Garden Nature trail parking area, walk 0.3 miles west along the paved road to an old, closed road on the left (GPS: N33°55.57200' / N115°56.15760'). Follow the old road south between two small volcanic cones. For the first 1.3 miles, the trail remains fairly level and is generally easy to follow. It crosses several washes marked by rock cairns. If you become temporarily lost, head toward the highest point on the southern horizon. In so doing, you'll eventually cross the trail when it becomes more distinct on the alluvial fan.

At 1.6 miles the trail crosses a wash and begins a steep 0.7-mile ascent to the mine. This extremely steep, rocky trail is washed out in a couple of places but well defined as a hiking route. From below, the uppermost mine site is hidden from view, but it sits in a notch in the left-hand (south) canyon. This 1930s mine contains a considerable amount of debris: metal, timbers, rusted pipe, rock walls, mine adits, tanks, and cable. Please do not disturb or remove any of these historic artifacts.

The mine is located near the top of a pass that drops southward into Fried Liver Wash. It provides a spectacular view to the north, particularly in the evening as the setting sun lights up Pinto Basin beneath the imposing mass of the Pinto Range.

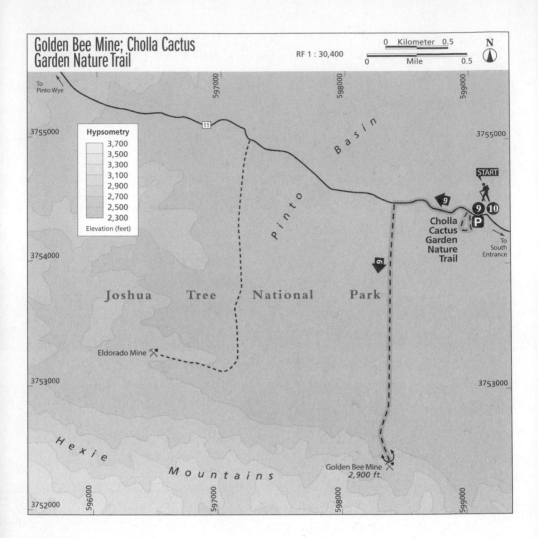

Golden Bee Mine; Cholla Cactus Garden Nature Trail

RF 1 : 30,400

Miles and Directions

0.3 The unsigned trailhead is on PR 11.

1.6 The trail crosses a wash and begins a steep climb to the mine.

2.3 Arrive at Golden Bee Mine (2,900 feet).

4.6 Return to the trailhead.

10 Cholla Cactus Garden Nature Trail

Here's an unusually dense stand of the distinctive "jumping" cholla cactus. The nature trail lies on the lower edge of the transition from Mojave Desert to Colorado Desert.

See map on page 36.
Start: 19 miles south of Twentynine Palms and 20 miles north of the Cottonwood Visitor Center.
Distance: 0.25-mile loop.
Approximate hiking time: Less than 30 minutes.

Difficulty: Easy.
Trail surface: Dirt path.
Seasons: October through April.
Maps: Trails Illustrated Joshua Tree National Park; USGS Fried Liver Wash.
Trail contact: Joshua Tree National Park (see appendix D).

Finding the trailhead: From California Highway 62 in Twentynine Palms, take Utah Trail south 4 miles to the North Entrance of the park; continue on Park Route 12 south 4.8 miles to the Pinto Y intersection. Turn left onto Park Route 11. The Cholla Cactus Garden parking area is on the right near mile marker 10, 6.3 miles south of the intersection. GPS: N33 55.532' / W115 55.28'

A dense stand of cholla cactus on the nature trail above Pinto Basin marks the northern end of the Colorado (Sonoran) Desert.

The Hike

This massive array of cholla, a common species of the Colorado (Sonoran) Desert, is impressive even when it is not in bloom. From mid- to late February to mid-March, there is intense bee activity at the garden. Those with sensitivity or phobias about bees should avoid visiting during the pollination season.

This is a self-guided trail with brochures explaining the numbers posted on the trail. But even without a pamphlet for interpretation, the density of the cholla, which extend well beyond the fenced edge of the garden, is impressive.

The views of the Hexie Mountains, the Pinto Range, and the Pinto Basin contribute to making the Cholla Cactus Garden a spectacular spot on the edge of this southern desert region.

11 Pleasant Valley to El Dorado Mine/Pinto Basin

This is a mostly downhill point-to-point hike, with opportunities for side trips to two mine sites, the Hexahedron and the El Dorado. The route begins in Pleasant Valley, crosses a low pass in the Hexie Mountains, and ends up in the Pinto Basin. Due to its trailless nature, this hike should only be undertaken by those skilled in cross-country desert navigation.

Start: About 19 miles south of Twentynine Palms.
Distance: 7.7 miles one way.
Approximate hiking time: 3 to 5 hours.
Difficulty: Moderate.
Trail surface: Rocky dirt path, sandy wash.

Seasons: October through May.
Maps: Trails Illustrated Joshua Tree National Park; USGS Malapai Hill and Fried Liver Wash.
Trail contact: Joshua Tree National Park (see appendix D).

Finding the trailhead: From the park visitor center in Twentynine Palms, go south on Utah Trail 8.2 miles to the Pinto Y intersection. Stay to the right on Park Route 12 and drive another 5.1 miles to Geology Tour Road (signed squaw tank at the junction). (From the other direction, this turnoff is 15.1 miles southeast of the town of Joshua Tree.) Turn left (south) on Geology Tour Road (washboard dirt) and drive 7.1 miles to the Pleasant Valley Backcountry Board, on the left side of Geology Tour Road in the one-way loop section in Pleasant Valley. GPS: N33°55.41720' / W116°03.24780'

For a car shuttle: At the Pinto Y intersection bear left on Park Route 11. Drive south to the pullout on the right just northwest of milepost 8. GPS: N33 55.937 / W115 57.397'

The Hike

This interesting point-to-point excursion of nearly 8 miles starts in Pleasant Valley along the upper Fried Liver Wash and the southern base of the Hexie Mountains,

The remains of the El Dorado Mine (elevation 2,650 feet).

ending up in the northwestern edge of the vast Pinto Basin. The trip presents an opportunity to explore the sizable El Dorado Mine site. The hike should only be done by those skilled in backcountry navigation.

The hike begins in a dry lake bed, which can be clearly delineated by walking up the sidehill to the north 100 feet or so before returning to the trail. At 0.3 mile a left-hand turn heads toward the hills. Stay to the right on the main traveled trail heading east.

Within another 0.2 mile Joshua trees are first seen along the trail. At 1.5 miles the trail passes by an old wooden post with no sign. Soon the trail and Fried Liver Wash become one and the same. At 2.5 miles a fence crosses the wash next to a hillside to the left. Turn left (north) and follow the fence line for about 0.2 mile to an old iron gatepost. Follow the trail leading uphill to the right. After another 0.1 mile you'll come to a trail junction in a flat; take the right-hand fork, which continues east in a small valley lined with Joshua trees. For a side trip, take the left-hand fork to the Hexahedron Mine.

At 3.8 miles the trail drops into a rough, rocky ravine, climbing out of it after another 0.1 mile. The gradual ascent continues for another 0.2 mile to a 3,170-foot pass overlooking the Pinto Basin to the east. After another 0.1 mile the trail all but disappears in the rock-strewn gully. Follow the wash down.

After 0.2 mile a small mine adit appears on the left, one of countless such holes in these hills. At this point the wash becomes sandier and easier to negotiate. Here

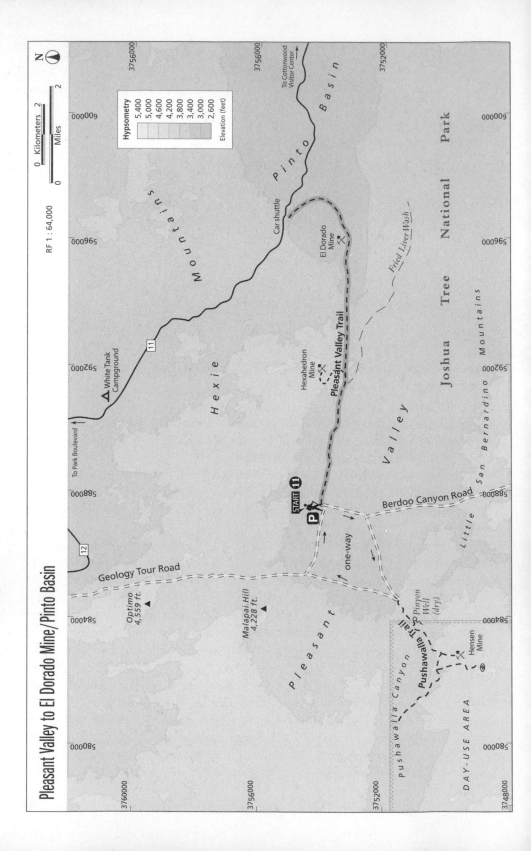

Pleasant Valley to El Dorado Mine/Pinto Basin

RF 1 : 64,000

and there a rusty water pipe sticks out. As the wash drops, the canyon opens up to ever-expanding views of Pinto Basin. After another 0.6 mile the wash widens, becoming more braided and difficult to walk down. At 5.7 miles the wash trail passes the El Dorado Mine. A single leaning building on the right looks as though a good puff of wind would blow it down. The huge piles of tailings give moot evidence that this mine produced the largest number of different minerals of any in the park.

If the El Dorado Mine is your destination and you've not arranged for a car shuttle, return the way you came for an 11.4 mile round-trip—a full day indeed. To continue the point-to-point hike, walk down the wash another 0.5 mile, gradually curving left (northward) around the base of the hill. Keep going another 1.5 miles north to northwest to an old mining road below the Tripples (Silver Bell) Mine, which leads to the parking area immediately northwest of milepost 8 on PR 11.

Miles and Directions

0.0 Start at the Pleasant Valley Backcountry Board.

0.3 The trail splits—stay right.

2.5 Where the fence crosses the wash, turn left (north).

2.8 Stay right at the trail junction with the Hexahedron Mine trail.

4.1 The trail tops a pass at 3,170 feet.

5.7 Arrive at the El Dorado Mine (2,650 feet).

7.7 Reach the end point of the hike at PR 11.

12 Hexahedron Mine

After a 3-mile hike down Fried Liver Wash, the mining-history enthusiast will enjoy exploring what remains of this old mine site. Even the nonhistorian will be thrilled by the view from the lofty aerie in the Hexie Mountains.

Start: 19 miles south of Twentynine Palms.
Distance: 8.4 miles out and back.
Approximate hiking time: 3 to 5 hours.
Difficulty: Moderately strenuous.
Trail surface: Rocky dirt path, sandy wash.

Seasons: October through May.
Maps: Trails Illustrated Joshua Tree National Park; USGS Malapai Hill.
Trail contact: Joshua Tree National Park (see appendix D).

Finding the trailhead: From the park visitor center in Twentynine Palms, go south on Utah Trail 8.2 miles to the Pinto Y intersection. Stay to the right on Park Route 12 for 5.1 miles to Geology Tour Road, which begins 15.1 miles southeast of the town of Joshua Tree. Turn left (south) on Geology Tour Road, which is signed SQUAW TANK at the turnoff. The Pleasant Valley Backcountry Board/trailhead is on the left after 7.1 miles. GPS: N33°55.41720' / W116°03.24780'

Hexahedron Mine shaft.

The Hike

From the Pleasant Valley Backcountry Board, this trail heads east in Pleasant Valley, along the foot of the Hexie Mountains across a dry lake bed. The rough-hewn Hexie Mountains rise to the immediate north. At 0.3 mile the trail splits; keep to the right. Old mine diggings can be seen on the hillside to the north. Soon the stark openness of the dry lake bed is moderated by a few Joshua trees near the trail.

At 1.5 miles the trail passes a wooden post with no sign. The trail then enters the head of Fried Liver Wash, dropping very gradually to the southeast. A fence crosses the wash at 2.5 miles. Take a left here and follow the fence north for about 0.2 mile to an old iron gatepost where a trail continues uphill to the right. Follow the trail another 0.1 mile onto a flat containing a trail junction. At this point the trail leading up to the mine can be clearly seen on the hillside to the north. Turn left and climb the rough, rocky trail another 1.4 miles to the Hexahedron Mine.

A roofless stone house stands guard near the mine adit, offering magnificent vistas of monzogranite quartz mounds northward. The main adit lies a short distance beyond, at the end of the trail. Retrace your route to complete this 8.4-mile round-trip. On the way back down, you'll be able to clearly see the outline of the dry lake bed.

For those staying overnight, there are good campsites near the upper reaches of Fried Liver Wash.

Hexahedron Mine

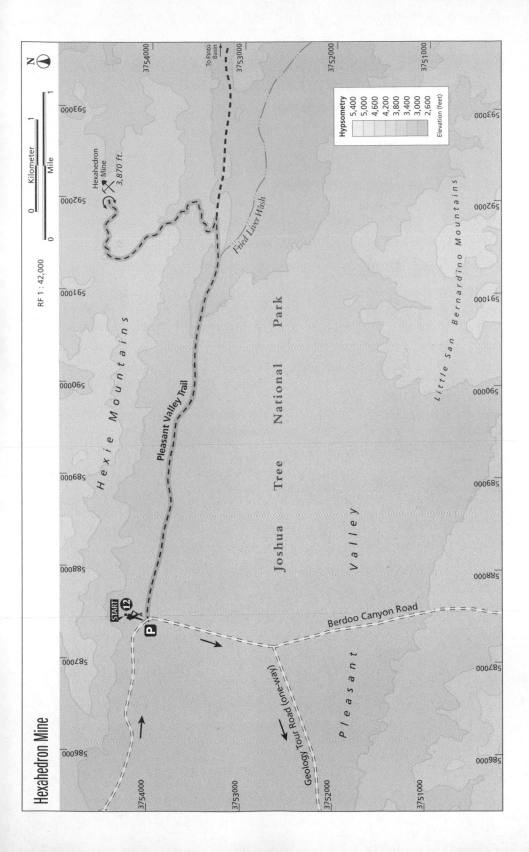

Miles and Directions

0.0 Start at the Pleasant Valley Backcountry Board (3,250 feet).

0.3 The trail splits—stay to the right (east).

2.5 Go north at the Fried Liver Wash fence crossing.

2.8 At the trail junction, take the trail on the left.

3.8 This is the high point of the trail (3,890 feet).

4.2 Arrive at Hexahedron Mine (3,870 feet).

8.4 Return to the trailhead.

13 Sand Dunes

Although the name is misleading (these are really hills, not dunes), this flat hike into the Pinto Basin gives you a sense of the wind's power to alter terrain in the desert.

Start: 13.5 miles north of Cottonwood Visitor Center.
Distance: 2.5 miles out and back.
Approximate hiking time: 1 to 3 hours.
Difficulty: Easy.
Trail surface: Dirt route.

Seasons: January through April.
Maps: Trails Illustrated Joshua Tree National Park; USGS Pinto Mountain.
Trail contact: Joshua Tree National Park (see appendix D).

Humble sand hills with the Pinto Mountains rising in the background.

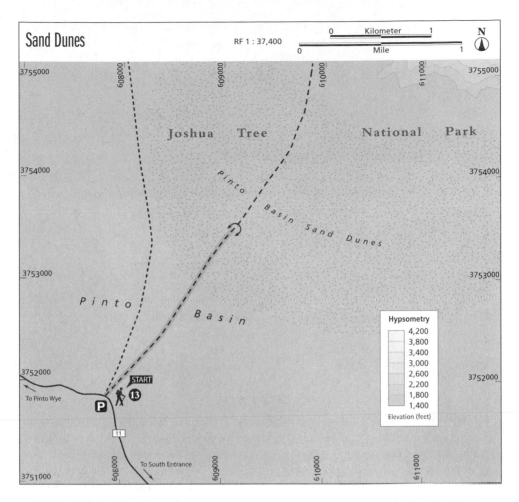

Sand Dunes

RF 1 : 37,400

Hypsometry

| 4,200 |
| 3,800 |
| 3,400 |
| 3,000 |
| 2,600 |
| 2,200 |
| 1,800 |
| 1,400 |

Elevation (feet)

Finding the trailhead: The route takes off from the Turkey Flats Backcountry Board, which is on the east side of Park Route 11, 16.2 miles south of the Pinto Y intersection and 13.5 miles north of the Cottonwood Visitor Center. GPS: N33°54.11460' / W115°50.08320'

The Hike

From the Turkey Flats Backcountry Board, head northeast on a line toward the high point on the distant horizon, 3,983-foot Pinto Mountain. The sand dunes can be seen about a mile away as a low-lying dark ridge or mound. Actually, these are not true sand dunes. The blowing sand collects on the face of a low gravel ridge, thus giving the appearance of a dune.

Begin by heading 0.2 mile up a large wash, which leads to a sand bowl. Continue northeasterly for another mile across a creosote-brittlebush flat to the sand dunes. This is a delightful place to visit during winter and, especially, spring, when primrose and other wildflowers are in bloom. Spend some quiet time here, wandering along this windswept uplift of sand, reflecting on how the ever-present desert winds have both created and kept in place these dunes over thousands of years.

To return, simply walk toward the highest point to the southwest, which is the crest of the Hexie Mountains, and you'll soon end up back at the backcountry board on PR 11.

14 Pushawalla Plateau/Canyon

This is an adventuresome day trip to the Pushawalla Plateau in the Little San Bernardino Mountains. Along the way you will enjoy seeing remnants of the mining era, hidden canyons, and expansive vistas to the Salton Sea and beyond. It's not a trip for those unskilled at backcountry navigation in the desert.

Start: About 27.5 miles south of Twentynine Palms.
Distance: 10.2 miles out and back.
Approximate hiking time: 5 to 7 hours for the long trip; 3 to 5 for the hike to the pass.
Difficulty: Strenuous.

Trail surface: Rocky wash, rocky trail, cross-country route.
Seasons: October through May.
Maps: Trails Illustrated Joshua Tree National Park; USGS Malapai Hill.
Trail contact: Joshua Tree National Park (see appendix D).

Finding the trailhead: From the park visitor center in Twentynine Palms, go south on Utah Trail 8.2 miles to the Pinto Y intersection. Stay to the right on Park Route 12 and drive another 5.1 miles to the signed Geology Tour Road (four-wheel drive recommended). (From the other direction, the turnoff is 15.1 miles southeast of the town of Joshua Tree.) Turn left (south) on Geology Tour Road (four-wheel drive recommended). The unsigned trailhead is 10.2 miles south next to the 15km post. Park at the Pinyon Well parking area and begin the hike up the wash. GPS: N33°54.04380' / W116°05.17320'

The Hike

This is an interesting hike with several side excursions into a remote and lightly used region of the park. All of the variations are out and back. They include going up "Pinyon Well" canyon to Pushawalla Pass, side-tripping up to Pushawalla Plateau, and dropping into the upper stretches of Pushawalla Canyon. These hikes are suggested only for those with skills in backcountry navigation, as the trails are not maintained.

The trail starts up a wash near the mouth of the Pinyon Well canyon, which drains east from Pushawalla Pass. The country is characterized by scattered juniper and Joshua trees, punctuated with spires of columnar rocks overlooking the canyon. The wash forks at 0.3 mile; stay to the right.

The wash widens just below Pushawalla Pass at 2.3 miles.

At 0.8 mile the canyon narrows just below the remains of a water trough and concrete foundations at Pinyon Well. A mine shaft is fenced off for public safety. At 1 mile (3,880 feet) a rock slide blocks the canyon; cut left on a use trail that quickly leads back to the wash. Look here for the remnants of the original asphalt roadway built by the miners.

At 1.2 miles the canyon again forks; stay left up the main wash. At 1.6 miles a piñon-juniper wash dotted with Joshua trees enters from the left (south) at 4,140 feet. For an expansive view of the canyon, take a 0.2-mile walk up the open wash to where heavy brush makes further hiking difficult.

At 1.9 miles the wash forks with the trail to Pushawalla Pass continuing to the left. At 2.2 miles the wash is again blocked by a rock slide, which can be avoided by taking the use trail to the left. At 2.4 miles (4,400 feet) the wash again forks; the smaller wash to the right is the route to Pushawalla Pass. Turn around here for a total out-and-back hike of 5.6 miles.

For a 0.6-mile side trip to some historic mining ruins (shown on the topo map), head up the left-hand wash at mile 2.4. After about 0.1 mile, climb toward the right-hand canyon on the right side of the draw. Soon you'll see the largely overgrown mining road up ahead. Follow it another 0.2 mile to the two roofless rock houses sitting just above a wet spring. Retrace your steps back to the right-hand fork, which climbs up the wash another 0.4 mile to 4,660-foot Pushawalla Pass at the head of Pushawalla Canyon. The pass is marked by an iron-post gate. Hold onto your hat, for

Pushawalla Plateau/Canyon

RF 1 : 64,000

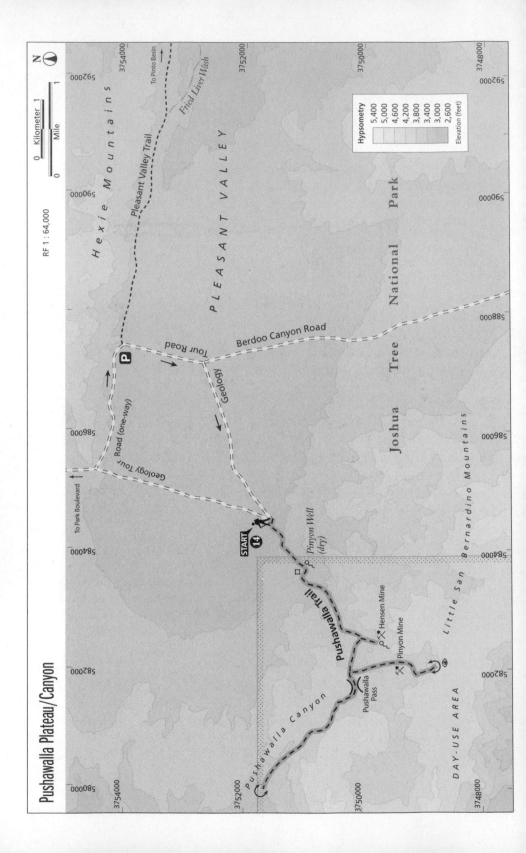

N

0 Kilometer 1
0 Mile 1

Hypsometry
5,400
5,000
4,600
4,200
3,800
3,400
3,000
2,600
Elevation (feet)

Hexie Mountains

To Pinto Basin

Pleasant Valley Trail

Fried Liver Wash

PLEASANT VALLEY

Berdoo Canyon Road

Geology Tour Road

P

Geology Tour Road (one-way)

To Park Boulevard

START 14

Pinyon Well (dry)

Pushawalla Trail

Hensen Mine

Pinyon Mine

Joshua Tree National Park

Little San Bernardino Mountains

Pushawalla Canyon

Pushawalla Pass

DAY-USE AREA

the pass is truly a classic high-desert wind funnel, decorated by piñon-juniper and live oak. If the pass is your goal, backtrack to complete your 6.2-mile round-trip.

Pushawalla Plateau

An old mining trail takes off to the south uphill about 50 yards east of Pushawalla Pass; several rock cairns mark the spot. The trail is quite steep in places but easy to follow. At 0.8 mile the trail passes by mining remains, including a rock foundation (5,120 feet). This is potentially a hazardous area because of unsecured vertical mine shafts nearby. The trail begins to fade here, but simply continue straight, angling upward to the left another 0.2 mile to the 5,200-foot crest of the Pushawalla Plateau ridge. Joshua trees and rock mounds characterize the landscape. Savor the spectacular views southward to the Salton Sea and in every direction in these remote Little San Bernardino Mountains. Seldom-visited ridges and canyons radiate below, and there is always the wind to keep you company.

Pushawalla Canyon

If time and energy permit, drop into the head of Pushawalla Canyon, where Joshua trees grow out of the wide, sandy bottom. To get there from the pass, walk around the right side of the iron gate and descend the trail on the left side of the gully to the broad wash. The canyon deepens as it drops, thereby enriching its sense of solitude. You'll lose 400 feet in the first 0.5 mile, so gauge your time accordingly for the return leg of this out-and-back adventure.

Miles and Directions

0.0 Start at the Pinyon Well trailhead.

0.8 Arrive at the Pinyon Well site.

1.2 Where the canyon forks, stay left up the main wash.

2.4–3.0 Take the left-hand fork for a side trip to the Hensen Well Mill site.

3.4 Arrive at Pushawalla Pass.

4.4 Arrive at Pushawalla Plateau.

5.4–6.4 A side trip down Pushawalla Canyon can be taken.

10.2 Return to the Pinyon Well trailhead.

Options: An overnight trip is not recommended here because the day-use area extends several more miles down Pushawalla Canyon—and because a point-to-point hike all the way down Pushawalla Canyon to the Dillon Road would require an inordinately long car shuttle. However, if distance and shuttle time are not obstacles, this long point-to-point route is an adventurous option. At this writing there is no end-of-the-road parking area at Pushawalla Canyon Road, which ends at the park boundary. However, the National Park Service does have plans to put in a backcountry board and parking area at this location.

Also for the adventurous hiker, the Pushawalla Canyon–Blue Cut loop provides a long 15-mile day trip or more moderate overnighter with a backpack camp in lower Pushawalla or upper Blue Cut Canyon outside of the day-use area. The basic route involves descending Pushawalla Canyon about 3.5 miles below the pass, turning right up Blue Cut Canyon for about 2 miles to the pass, then dropping eastward into Pleasant Valley for the return trip to the Pinyon Well trailhead on Geology Tour Road.

15 Keys View Loop/Inspiration Peak

What a view! From either the loop or the peak, you can see forever on a clear day. With the usual air pollution, however, you see a lot less. On the loop you can also pick up information on the geology of Joshua Tree National Park and the increase of air pollution in the desert basins.

Start: 23.3 miles southwest of Twentynine Palms.
Distance: 1.75 miles with loop and out and back to peak.
Approximate hiking time: Less than 30 minutes for the loop; an hour or so for the peak.
Difficulty: Easy; moderate for peak hike.

Trail surface: Dirt path.
Seasons: October through June.
Maps: Trails Illustrated Joshua Tree National Park; USGS Keys View.
Trail contact: Joshua Tree National Park (see appendix D).

From Inspiration Peak (5,550 feet) looking north to the Wonderland of Rocks.

RF 1 : 51,750

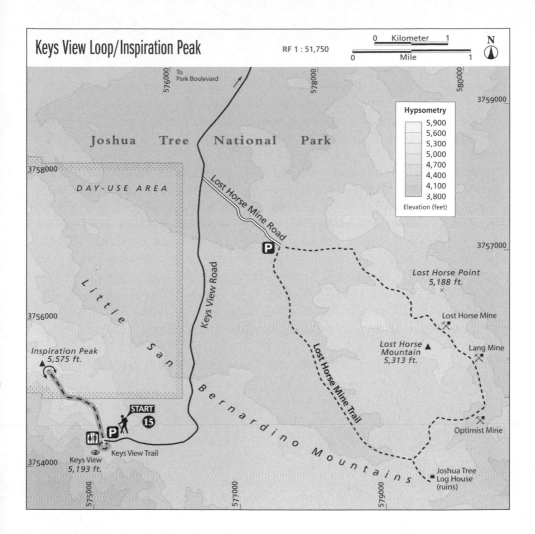

Finding the trailhead: From California Highway 62 in the town of Joshua Tree, take Park Boulevard south 1 mile to where it becomes Quail Springs Road; continue 4.3 miles to the West Entrance of the park. Follow Park Route 12 for 11.2 miles to Keys View Road (Park Route 13), which continues to the right (south). Turn south on Keys View; go 5.8 miles to the end of the road. GPS: N33 55.622 / W116 11.252

The Hike

This clear, paved, barrier-free path to Keys View Loop is the highest trail in the park accessible by a paved road. You can count on a brisk breeze, so bring your windbreaker. The view point is on the crest of the Little San Bernardino Mountains. As such, it provides an expansive view of the Coachella Valley and the San Bernardino Range to the west. Unfortunately, the view is all too often obscured by pollution from the Los Angeles Basin. Information boards contrasting smog levels give the viewer a good idea of how air pollution affects visibility at differing distances. The smog also endangers the biological integrity of the park itself.

The park has plans for exhibits at Keys View that will discuss earthquakes and point out landmarks. Until then your park map will help orient you to the view.

A short side trip to Inspiration Peak makes a nice addition for those who like to get even higher. A hiker symbol marks the trailhead on the right (north) side of the parking area at Keys View. The somewhat steep, rocky trail is well worn and in good condition. Nearly 400 feet are gained to a false summit in the first 0.5 mile.

Look carefully for the trail continuing to the right. It drops 100 feet into a saddle and then climbs around the left side, gaining 120 feet in the next 0.25 mile. Keys View sits far below to the south, as do the Coachella Valley and prominent peaks of the higher San Bernardino Range. The added perspective gained on the steep canyons and high ridges makes this steep, short climb more than worthwhile.

An easily followed use trail continues another 0.1 mile northwest along the main crest until it reaches a mound of large boulders. The Inspiration Peak hike can be extended by scrambling over the rocks and dropping into another saddle containing a small storage shed. Climbing cross-country up the ridgeline to the next high point offers even broader views of the park stretching west and north to the Wonderland of Rocks.

From Inspiration Peak, double-back 0.75 mile on the trail leading back down to the Keys View parking area.

16 Lost Horse Mine Loop

This loop trip includes two mines, a mountain, unusual ruins of a Joshua tree cabin, and expansive vistas of the Wonderland of Rocks, Malapai Hill, and Pleasant Valley. Only those skilled at backcountry desert navigation should undertake the full loop.

Start: 23 miles southwest of Twentynine Palms.
Distance: 7.8-mile loop.
Approximate hiking time: 5 to 6 hours.
Difficulty: Strenuous.
Trail surface: Mostly dirt trail.

Seasons: October through May.
Maps: Trails Illustrated Joshua Tree National Park; USGS Keys View.
Trail contact: Joshua Tree National Park (see appendix D).

Finding the trailhead: Drive south on Keys View Road, which begins 18 miles southeast of the town of Joshua Tree via Park Boulevard and Quail Springs Road, or 20 miles southwest of the Oasis Visitor Center at Twentynine Palms by way of Park Route 12. Continue south on Keys View Road for 2.6 miles to the signed Lost Horse Mine Road (GPS: N33 57.050' / W116 9.593'). Turn left (southeast) and drive to the Lost Horse Mine parking area/trailhead, which is at the end of this 1.1-mile dirt road.

The remains of an early-day Joshua tree log house.

The Hike

This multifaceted hike offers something for every hiking enthusiast: a moderate climb to a large mining complex, then a more strenuous trail for those wishing to experience a bit of adventurous route-finding. There are also side trips to several high panoramic points. The loop trip—follow it clockwise—is recommended only for those skilled in backcountry navigation; others may want to turn around at the Lost Horse Mine for a moderate out and back of four to five hours' duration.

The clear and wide but somewhat rocky trail climbs moderately for 1 mile across high desert swales of juniper, yucca, a few stunted Joshua trees, and nolina (commonly called bear grass), a member of the agave family often mistaken for yucca because of its long spearlike leaves. At 2 miles the trail reaches the lower end of the Lost Horse Mine. This is the largest, essentially intact, historic mining site in the park, and you could easily spend several hours here observing rock buildings, mine shafts, a large wooden stamp mill, and a winch above the mill that was used to lower miners and equipment into the mine. The largest mine shaft, some 500 feet deep, is covered. However, other smaller ones remain unsecured on the hillsides, so exercise caution when wandering around this site.

This was one of the most profitable mines in the park. A German miner named Frank Diebold made the first strike. He was later bought out by prospector Johnny Lang, who happened onto the strike in 1893 while searching for a lost horse. He and his partners began developing the mine two years later. Their process involved crushing ore at the mill, then mixing it with quicksilver (mercury), which bonded

0   Kilometer   1

0   Mile   1

N

Joshua   Tree   National   Park

To Park
Boulevard

Hypsometry
5,900
5,600
5,300
5,000
4,700
4,400
4,100
3,800
Elevation (feet)

576000

578000

580000

3759000

3758000

DAY-USE AREA

Lost Horse Mine Road

START
16

3757000

Lost Horse Point
5,188 ft.
×

Lost Horse Mine

3756000

L i t t l e   S a n

Keys View Road

Lost Horse
Mountain ▲
5,313 ft.

Lang Mine

Inspiration Peak
▲ 5,575 ft.

Lost Horse Mine Trail

B e r n a r d i n o   M o u n t a i n s

Optimist Mine

Keys View Trail

3754000

Keys View
5,193 ft.

Joshua Tree
Log House
(ruins)

575000

577000

579000

with the gold so that it could be separated from the ore rock. After visiting the mine, you can double-back the way you came for a moderate 4-mile round-trip.

For a bird's-eye view of the Lost Horse Mine and its surroundings, hike north 0.2 mile on the trail that climbs above the fenced-off stamp mill. A 0.1-mile use trail continues up to Lost Horse Point (5,188 feet), which affords a magnificent panorama of surrounding basins and peaks, including the Wonderland of Rocks to the north. From here you can see a trail running southeast to a pass. Using care on the loose rocks, drop down this trail and walk 0.2 mile to the pass to climb 5,313-foot Lost Horse Mountain. From the pass, climb southwest 0.3 mile up the ridge, gaining 200 feet, to the long ridgetop that forms the summit of the mountain. There is a faint use trail that is easier seen coming down than going up, but climbing is easy on or off the use trail.

To continue the loop drop back to the pass and continue dropping steeply to the southeast on a rough and rocky trail 0.4 mile to the unsecured Lang Mine. The trail ends here; continue on a well-defined trail that contours another 0.2 mile on the hillside to a small flat spot marked by a large cairn. This is the end of the trail and the start of the short cross–country segment. Instead of dropping any farther, angle sharply upward and to the right (southwest) to the closest ridge, wrapping around the small hill to the right for about 0.1 mile. From here the stone chimney, tailings, and trail of the Optimist Mine can be seen downhill and across the gully to the south.

Drop down to the chimney in 0.1 mile and pick up the easy-to-follow trail, which winds uphill and to the right. The trail travels westward in and around several small hills and gullies 0.4 mile to a wooden post with the number 8. After another 0.4 mile the trail drops into a wide wash at about mile 4.4 in the loop trip.

Take an interesting short side trip to a Joshua tree log house by hiking up the wash to the first fork at 0.2 mile. Continue southeast on the left-hand fork another 0.2 mile to the cabin ruins, which are on the left side of the wash along with the faint remnants of an old mining road. This structure stands as a rustic reminder of why Joshua trees are so scarce in this heavily prospected mining district.

Return to the junction and continue northwest down either the trail or the wash, both of which end up on the Lost Horse Mine Road about 100 yards below the parking area. The trail provides firmer walking but at times disappears in the wash. When in doubt simply follow the wash—eventually you'll pick up the trail on one of its several crossings. The wash is bounded by low-lying ridges with the valley opening up to vistas of distant mountains to the northwest. Joshua trees become larger and more abundant on this return leg of the loop as the distance increases from the mining sites. Upon reaching the Lost Horse Mine Road, turn right and walk the remaining short distance to the parking area/trailhead.

Note: Those wishing to backpack and camp overnight on the loop route must start at the Juniper Flats Backcountry Board, 1.5 miles north of the turnoff to the Lost Horse Mine trail, 0.25 mile east of the parking area, thereby adding 3.5 miles to the loop. There are several good campsites near the junction of the trail and wash near mile 4 of the loop.

Miles and Directions

0.0 Begin at the Lost Horse Mine parking area/trailhead.

2.0 Arrive at Lost Horse Mine.

2.2 Arrive at Lost Horse Point.

2.4 Arrive at a pass southeast of the mine.

2.7 Reach Lost Horse Mountain (5,313 feet).

3.4 Arrive at Lang Mine.

3.6 Reach the end of the trail/beginning of the cross-country leg.

3.8 Arrive at Optimist Mine.

4.5 The trail enters and follows a wash.

4.9 You'll see the ruins of a Joshua tree log house.

7.8 This is the end of the loop.

17 California Riding and Hiking Trail: Keys View Road to Park Route 11

Here you'll find solitude in a busy region of the park, as well as sweeping vistas of Juniper Flats and the Pinto Basin. Two sections of the California Riding and Hiking Trail, largely downhill over a broad trail, can be hiked as a single unit of 11 miles as a point-to-point day hike, or broken into 6.5- and 4.4-mile one-way units.

Start: 15 miles southwest of Twentynine Palms.
Distance: 11.1 miles one way, with car shuttle.
Approximate hiking time: 4 to 6 hours.
Difficulty: Moderate.
Trail surface: Dirt path.

Seasons: October through April.
Maps: Trails Illustrated Joshua Tree National Park; USGS Keys View and Malapai Hill.
Trail contact: Joshua Tree National Park (see appendix D).

Finding the trailhead: From California Highway 62 in Twentynine Palms, take Utah Trail south 4 miles to the North Entrance of the park; continue on Park Route 12 for 15.8 miles to the Keys View Road left turn, which is at the Cap Rock Nature Trail. Turn left (southwest) on Keys View and continue 1.1 miles to the Juniper Flats Backcountry Board on your right. The trail itself crosses Keys View Road just to the north of the board parking area. A spur trail leads you to the main trail. GPS: N33°58.67340' / W116°09.89040'

For a car shuttle: For a partial trip, your pickup point is on Geology Tour Road, 10.2 miles down PR 12 from the North Entrance, on your left; the backcountry board and parking area are south on Geology Tour Road, 1.4 miles, on your right. GPS: N33°59.10480' / W116°04.93920'

For the longer hike, the pickup spot is on Park Route 11 near the Arch Rock Nature Trail and White Tank Campground. From the North Entrance go south on PR 12 for 4.8 miles to the Pinto Y junction; turn left on PR 11 and go south 2.3 miles to the Twin Tank Backcountry Board, on your right. GPS: N33°59.27520' / W116°01.34820'

The Hike

Whether done as one long hike or two short hikes, these outings provide an excellent tour of the central area of Joshua Tree National Park. The California Riding and Hiking Trail is largely sandy. These sections feature a fairly broad pathway; the final 4.4 miles are on a trail as wide as a city sidewalk. In spite of its title, there is minimal horse usage. We never saw a hoofprint on our hike.

The trail is well marked with arrowed signposts, and even features mile markers (mile 1 is on the slightly used portion starting near the North Entrance), so you always know where you are. Except for a gradual 250-foot rise in the first portion after Ryan Campground, the trail is nearly all downhill. This, combined with the easy footing, makes it possible to stroll along enjoying the scenery.

And the scenery is superb! From Keys View you cross the interior valley south of Ryan Mountain. Although you are not in a remote corner of the park, there is

The California R&H Trail near the White Tank Campground provides sweeping vistas of the Pinto Basin and Range to the east.

a definite sense of total solitude. Hiking through the valley and on down the ridge into Pleasant Valley, you'll enjoy a wide field of vision, unlike the wash and canyon hikes elsewhere in the park. The Little San Bernardinos rise to the right, and the Pinto Mountains loom larger in the distance to the east. The distinctive peaks of Ryan Mountain, Malapai Hill, the Hexie Range, and Crown Prince Lookout punctuate your trip.

The final section of the hike is the easiest portion of the Riding and Hiking Trail in the park. Many hikers park at either end and do it as an easy out and back, avoiding the hassle of the car shuttle. West to east, of course, the downhill slope is advantageous. And what a vista there is as you descend gradually toward the Pinto Basin stretching before you into the hazy distance. With only a bit of imagination, you can envision the early Pinto Basin inhabitants enjoying life around the lake that once lay in the grassy valley between the mountains. With a net loss of elevation of nearly 600 feet, the 4.4-mile section also gives you a relaxed opportunity to notice vegetation changes as you descend from the Mojave to the Colorado (Sonoran) Desert. The Joshua trees are numerous and large at your 4,500-foot commencement at Geology Tour Road. Gradually, they become more sparse and quite small, until they are nearly nonexistent. Instead, creosote dominates, and cholla cacti increase. By the end of the hike, you are in a new botanical environment.

If you have more time and energy, the Twin Tanks monzogranite region is immediately west of the backcountry board on PR 11. You can see the hulking granite

California Riding and Hiking Trail: Keys View Road to Park Route 11

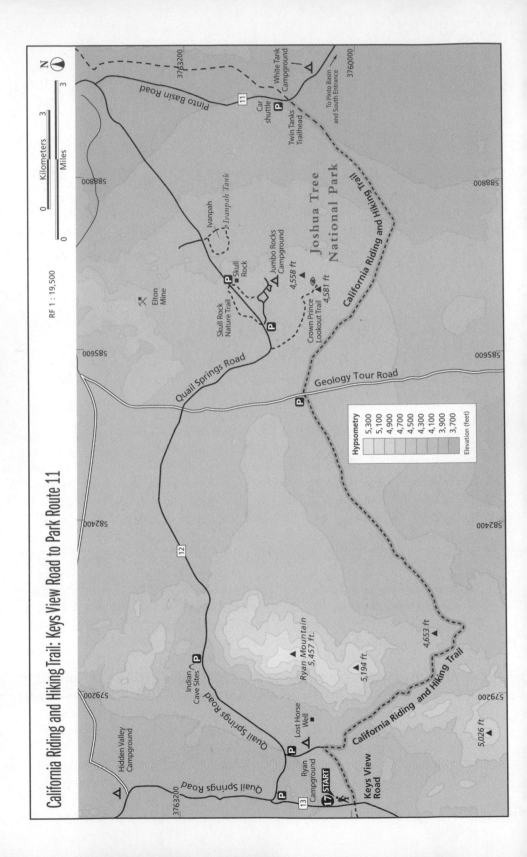

formations to the north of the trail as you approach the board. These looming forms are quite a bit larger than they appear, for they are hiding in a ravine, crouching below the horizon. A 1-mile hike west of the board will take you to this fanciful granite playground with curiously eroded caves, tunnels, and sculptures.

Note: In Joshua Tree the backcountry boards are not located exactly on the California Riding and Hiking Trail. In each case, the trail crosses the road slightly to the north or to the south of the board itself. The board structures are large enough for you to spot them above the desert vegetation, and feeder trails will lead you to or from the boards at the beginning and end of your hikes.

Miles and Directions

0.0–0.7 From the Juniper Flats Backcountry Board, the trail leads northeast toward Ryan Campground, then turns east.

1.5 Arrive at a saddle pass, the high point of the hike (4,540 feet).

2.5 The mine site is below the trail to the right. Fifty yards farther the trail goes right through prospectors' ruins.

6.5 Cross Geology Tour Road.

10.9 Arrive at PR 11.

11.1 The board and parking area are 0.2 mile north for an 11.1-mile one-way hike.

18 Arch Rock Nature Trail

This short nature walk features geology lessons, which are illustrated by the striking white granite formations that surround you. There's also an opportunity for a side trip to an old cattle tank that continues to provide a patch of greenery in the desert.

Start: 8.5 miles south of Twentynine Palms.
Distance: 0.3-mile loop.
Approximate hiking time: 30 minutes to 1 hour.
Difficulty: Easy nature trail.
Trail surface: Dirt path.

Seasons: October through April.
Maps: Trails Illustrated Joshua Tree National Park; USGS Malapai Hill.
Trail contact: Joshua Tree National Park (see appendix D).

Finding the trailhead: From California Highway 62 in Twentynine Palms, take Utah Trail south 4 miles to the North Entrance of the park; continue south on Park Route 12 for 4.8 miles to the Pinto Y intersection. Turn left at the Y onto Park Route 11 and go 2.8 miles to the White Tank Campground, on your left. Turn into the campground and follow the inconspicuous nature-trail sign to the trailhead, on the left immediately after the campground information board. GPS: N33 59.162 / W116 1.018'

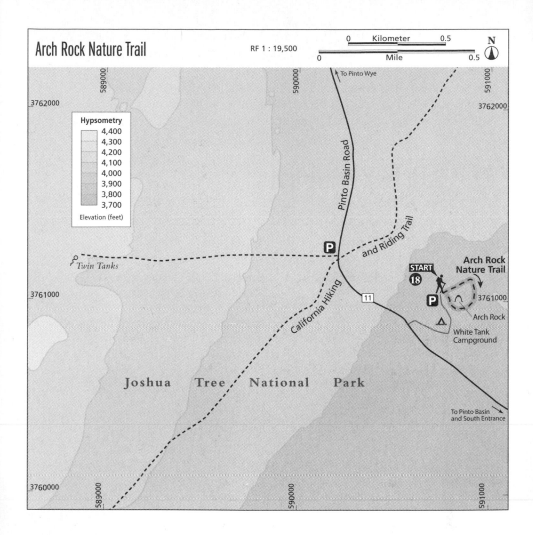

Arch Rock Nature Trail

RF 1 : 19,500

0   Kilometer   0.5

0   Mile   0.5

N

Hypsometry

4,400
4,300
4,200
4,100
4,000
3,900
3,800
3,700

Elevation (feet)

3762000

3762000

To Pinto Wye

Pinto Basin Road

and Riding Trail

Twin Tanks

Arch Rock
Nature Trail

START
18

3761000

California Hiking

11

Arch Rock

3761000

White Tank
Campground

Joshua   Tree   National   Park

To Pinto Basin
and South Entrance

3760000

The Hike

The focus of this nature trail is on the unique geology of the fascinating rock formations that abound in this area of the park. Informational signs present a sophisticated
series of geology lessons, far beyond the simplistic rock identification that usually
occurs on such a trail. The trail itself is an adventure in geology as it winds through
imaginative boulders to the famed Arch Rock.

A side trip from this rock through the slot to the northeast leads to the site of an
old cattle tank, which is no longer holding water but has created a habitat for birds
and other desert creatures.

◀   *The granite arch on the Arch Rock Nature Trail.*

The geology lesson covers the formation of igneous rock, the origins of White Tank granite, erosion, selective erosion, dikes, and faults. The remainder of your visit in the park will be greatly enhanced by this knowledge. For example, 1 mile west of White Tank Campground are the Twin Tanks. Like Arch Rock, these granite formations are gracefully sculpted by the forces of weather and are inviting to explore. Twin Tanks also has two partially buried old tank sites.

19 Skull Rock Nature Trail

This easy nature trail, located at the Jumbo Rocks Campground, winds through the fanciful rock formations that make this region of the park so distinctive.

Start: 12 miles south of Twentynine Palms.
Distance: 1.7-mile loop.
Approximate hiking time: 1 to 2 hours.
Difficulty: Easy.
Trail surface: Dirt path.

Seasons: October through April.
Maps: Trails Illustrated Joshua Tree National Park; USGS Malapai Hill.
Trail contact: Joshua Tree National Park (see appendix D).

This eroded monzogranite boulder gives Skull Rock Nature Trail its morbid name.

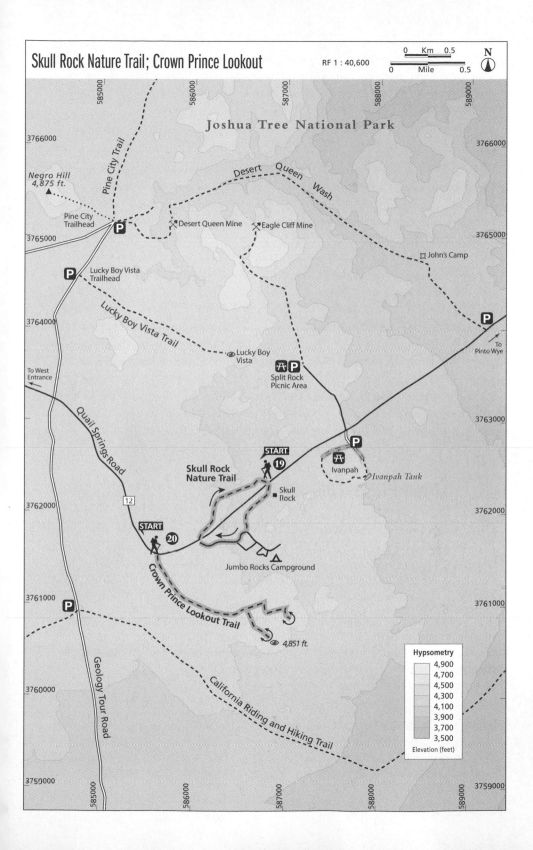

Skull Rock Nature Trail; Crown Prince Lookout

RF 1 : 40,600

0   Km   0.5

0   Mile   0.5

N

585000   586000   587000   588000   589000

Joshua Tree National Park

3766000

Pine City Trail

Negro Hill
4,875 ft.

Desert   Queen   Wash

Pine City
Trailhead

P

Desert Queen Mine

Eagle Cliff Mine

3765000

John's Camp

P   Lucky Boy Vista
Trailhead

P

3764000

Lucky Boy Vista Trail

To
Pinto Wye

Lucky Boy
Vista

Split Rock
Picnic Area

3763000

To West
Entrance

Quail Springs Road

P

12

START
19

**Skull Rock
Nature Trail**

Ivanpah

Ivanpah Tank

Skull
Rock

3762000

START
20

Jumbo Rocks Campground

Crown Prince Lookout Trail

3761000

P

4,851 ft.

Geology Tour Road

California Riding and Hiking Trail

3760000

Hypsometry

4,900
4,700
4,500
4,300
4,100
3,900
3,700
3,500

Elevation (feet)

3759000

585000   586000   587000   588000   589000

Finding the trailhead: From California Highway 62 in Twentynine Palms, take Utah Trail south 4 miles to the North Entrance of the park; continue on Park Route 12 for 4.8 miles to the Pinto Y intersection. Bear right, still on PR 12, and continue 3.8 miles to the signed Skull Rock Nature Trail trailhead. GPS: N33 59.87159.623' / W 116 3.597'

The Hike

This loop trail is divided by PR 12. The northern half of the loop begins at the Skull Rock sign on the highway and goes northward; at 0.7 mile it ends at the Jumbo Rocks Campground entrance. To pick up the rest of the trail from there, it is necessary to walk down through the campground (0.5 mile) to the end of loop E to get to the other half. This northern half of the loop has not recently been renovated by the park. Several signs are so weathered they are illegible. The trail is haphazardly marked with rocks and is not always clear. Although the eroded boulders are a spectacular sight, the information provided is not thematic. Basic geology, plant identification, and desert survival tips are intermixed. The park has plans to improve the signage.

Across the road, on the southern half of the loop, the signs are recent, more plentiful, and more instructive. They focus on desert diversity and the interconnectedness of the plants and animals that make this region their home. The famous, much-photographed Skull Rock sits at the entrance (or exit) of the southern loop, immediately adjacent to the road. From there, the trail winds southward 0.5 mile to the southern end of Jumbo Rocks Campground on the E loop. Hike up the campground road to pick up the northern loop opposite the campground entrance on PR 12.

20 Crown Prince Lookout

Named for its role as a World War II lookout, this high point above the desert floor still provides a vantage point for hikers, with views of Queen Valley, from Pushawalla Plateau to Queen Mountain, Twin Tanks, Arch Rock, and the Pinto Range.

See map on page 63.
Start: 12 miles south of Twentynine Palms.
Distance: 3 miles out and back.
Approximate hiking time: 2 to 3 hours.
Difficulty: Easy.
Trail surface: Sandy trail.

Seasons: October through April.
Maps: Trails Illustrated Joshua Tree National Park; USGS Malapai Hill.
Trail contact: Joshua Tree National Park (see appendix D).

Finding the trailhead: From California Highway 62 in Twentynine Palms, take Utah Trail south 4 miles to the North Entrance of the park; continue south on Park Route 12 for 4.8 miles to the Pinto Y intersection. Bear right and continue on PR 12 another 3.7 miles to Jumbo Rocks Campground. Park in the visitor lot at the entrance. GPS: N33°59.53620' / W116°04.06140'

The trail to Crown Prince Lookout leads clearly to the overlook jutting above the plateau in the distance.

The Hike

Walk west along the road shoulder 0.25 mile to the trailhead at the sharp curve in the road west of the campground. The trail is marked by six huge stones placed there to block vehicle access on this former jeep route. The trailhead is unsigned.

This easy hike follows a well-defined old jeep track up a broad sandy ridge. At 1.3 miles the trail splits at a Y. To the right the trail heads for a huge boulder pile; do not be intimidated, for the trail curves around to an adjacent promontory and does not climb the peak. From the vista point, you can see the valleys to the east and the vast White Tank granite formations that lie between here and the Pinto Mountains. For the adventuresome hiker, wend your way to the top of Crown Prince to see the remains of the World War II observation post, the lookout for which the outing is named. It's an interesting historical aspect of the hike.

Back at the Y, the trail now on the right is also a gentle 0.2-mile track. It ends in a broad, sandy turnaround. A footpath continues to the right of a more modest boulder pile and ends at an old mine site.

The walk back to PR 12 is entirely downhill.

21 Ryan Mountain

Unlike most other peaks in the park, Ryan Mountain is located right by a paved road, so there's no long warm-up before the climb begins. When you reach the summit, you'll be rewarded with a panoramic view of the park.

Start: About 20 miles southwest of Twentynine Palms.
Distance: 3 miles out and back.
Approximate hiking time: 4 to 5 hours.
Difficulty: Strenuous.
Trail surface: Dirt and rock path.

Seasons: October through May.
Maps: Trails Illustrated Joshua Tree National Park; USGS Indian Cove and Keys View.
Trail contact: Joshua Tree National Park (see appendix D).

Finding the trailhead: From California Highway 62 in Joshua Tree, drive south on Park Boulevard for 1 mile. It changes to Quail Springs Road; continue 4 miles to the West Entrance of the park. Follow Park Route 12 for 12.5 miles to Ryan Mountain Trailhead, on your right (south). The signed parking area is 2.1 miles east of the junction with Keys View Road. GPS: N34°00.15720' / W116°08.14980'

The granite boulders of Wonderland of Rocks stretch off to the north from Ryan Mountain.

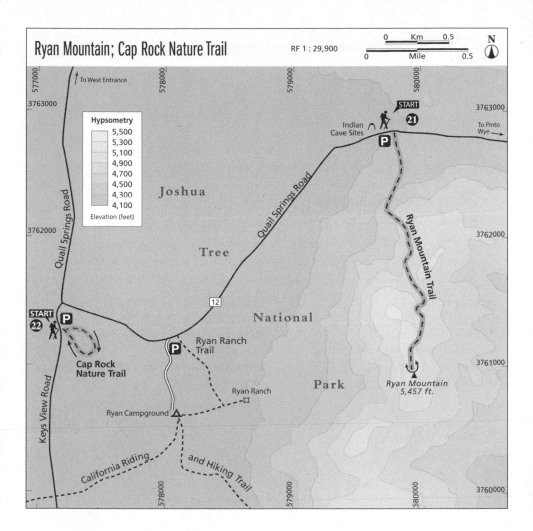

Ryan Mountain; Cap Rock Nature Trail

RF 1 : 29,900

0   Km   0.5
0   Mile   0.5
N

Hypsometry

	5,500
	5,300
	5,100
	4,900
	4,700
	4,500
	4,300
	4,100

Elevation (feet)

To West Entrance

START 21

Indian Cave Sites

To Pinto Wye

Ryan Mountain Trail

Joshua

Tree

Quail Springs Road

National

12

START 22

Cap Rock Nature Trail

Keys View Road

Ryan Ranch Trail

Ryan Ranch

Ryan Campground

Park

Ryan Mountain 5,457 ft.

California Riding

and Hiking Trail

The Hike

The trail leaves from the parking area through a massive boulder gate of White Tank granite sculpted by selective erosion. This well-signed official park trail is quite a display of rock workmanship. Steeper portions of the trail feature stair-steps artfully constructed from plentiful native rocks, so it's easy walking up and there's no skidding going down. The trail winds around the hill by the trailhead and takes a relatively gentle slope to the peak.

If you have spent several days walking nature trails, visiting mine sites, and hiking canyon washes, this peak climb provides a welcome aerial view of where you've been in the central portion of the park. On your return, don't miss the Indian Cave sites at the western end of the parking area. A sign indicates their location. The fire-stained rock shelters provide a reminder of the centuries of use that this land has seen from human visitors.

Miles and Directions

0.0 Start at the trailhead.

0.1 Huge boulders frame the trail.

0.4 The trail begins a steep climb.

1.5 Reach the summit of Ryan Mountain.

3.0 Return to the trailhead.

22 Cap Rock Nature Trail

Here's a loop trip around a spectacular monzogranite formation on a hard-surfaced barrier-free path. Signs along the trail provide information about desert plants.

See map on page 67.
Start: 22 miles southwest of Twentynine Palms.
Distance: 0.4-mile loop.
Approximate hiking time: Less than 30 minutes.
Difficulty: Easy.

Trail surface: Hard surface, barrier-free.
Seasons: October through May.
Maps: Trails Illustrated Joshua Tree National Park; USGS Keys View.
Trail contact: Joshua Tree National Park (see appendix D).

Cap Rock, with its sporty visor, is a popular spot for rock climbers.

Finding the trailhead: From California Highway 62 in Joshua Tree, take the Park Boulevard exit south 1 mile, to where it turns into Quail Springs Road, and continue 4 miles to the West Entrance of the park. Continue on Park Route 12 for 15 miles to the right turn on Keys View Road. The Cap Rock parking area is on the left (east) side of road 0.1 mile from the intersection. GPS: N33 59.34859.924' / W116 9.827'

The Hike

This easy nature trail is paved and designed to accommodate wheelchairs. Numerous informational signs dot your route. The focus of the information is on the desert plants that grow around these fascinating quartz monzonite boulder piles. Cap Rock itself is nearby; frequent use by rock climbers makes this an interesting scene.

23 Lucky Boy Vista

This outing provides a vista of the Split Rock region of the park. The trail also takes you to the remains of the Elton Mine.

Start: 16 miles south of Twentynine Palms.
Distance: 2.5 miles out and back.
Approximate hiking time: 2 to 3 hours.
Difficulty: Easy.
Trail surface: Sandy trail.

Seasons: October through April.
Maps: Trails Illustrated Joshua Tree National Park; USGS Queen Mountain.
Trail contact: Joshua Tree National Park (see appendix D).

Finding the trailhead: From California Highway 62 in Twentynine Palms, take Utah Trail south 4 miles to the North Entrance of the park; continue on Park Route 12 for 4.8 miles to the Pinto Y intersection. Bear right and stay on PR 12 another 5.2 miles to the dirt road on your right (directly opposite Desert Queen Mine Road, which goes south). Turn north on the dirt road and go 0.8 mile to a gated road going east. Park there. GPS: N34°01.06920' / W116°04.94040'

The Hike

This relatively flat hike to the Elton Mine site is on a broad sandy jeep track, which is in better shape than the Desert Queen Mine Road you took to get here. The trail climbs gradually above a yucca and piñon boulder garden to the north. At 1 mile there is a gate; continue around it. Shortly afterward you will see the fenced-off mine shafts on your right. Just beyond the mine on a lofty plateau is a magnificent overlook of the Split Rock region of the park. For a short hike, this outing provides you with an opportunity for desert solitude, a great view, and a historic site.

The reverse view on the trip back to the car is equally spacious.

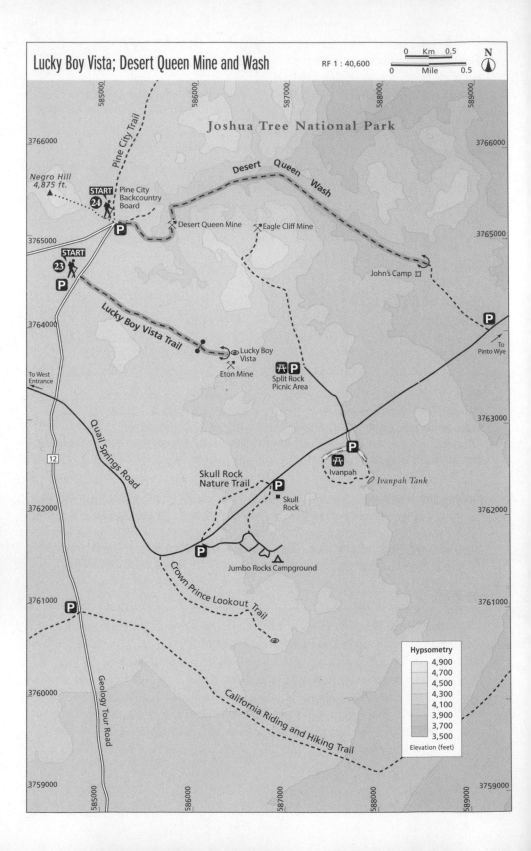

Lucky Boy Vista; Desert Queen Mine and Wash

RF 1 : 40,600

0   Km   0.5
0   Mile   0.5

N

585000

586000

587000

588000

589000

3766000

Joshua Tree National Park

3766000

Pine City Trail

Desert Queen Wash

Negro Hill
4,875 ft.

START
24

Pine City
Backcountry
Board

P

Desert Queen Mine

Eagle Cliff Mine

John's Camp

3765000

3765000

START
23

P

P
To Pinto Wye

Lucky Boy Vista Trail

3764000

Lucky Boy
Vista

Eton Mine

Split Rock
Picnic Area

P

To West
Entrance

3763000

Quail Springs Road

P

12

Skull Rock
Nature Trail

P

Ivanpah

Ivanpah Tank

3762000

Skull
Rock

3762000

P

Jumbo Rocks Campground

Crown Prince Lookout Trail

3761000

P

3761000

Geology Tour Road

California Riding and Hiking Trail

Hypsometry

4,900
4,700
4,500
4,300
4,100
3,900
3,700
3,500

Elevation (feet)

3760000

585000

586000

587000

588000

589000

3759000

3759000

24 Desert Queen Mine and Wash

The view of the Desert Queen Mine, the largest and longest-running mine in the park, from the overlook near the trailhead will tantalize you to explore farther down the wash, where traces of additional mines and miner settlements are located.

See map on page 70.
Start: 15 miles south of Twentynine Palms.
Distance: 4 miles out and back.
Approximate hiking time: 1 to 5 hours, depending on distance.
Difficulty: Easy (to overlook); moderate (to mine site and on down the wash).

Trail surface: Sandy trail.
Seasons: October through April.
Maps: Trails Illustrated Joshua Tree National Park; USGS Queen Mountain.
Trail contact: Joshua Tree National Park (see appendix D).

Finding the trailhead: From the visitor center in Twentynine Palms continue south on Utah Trail 8.2 miles to the Pinto Y intersection. Stay to the right on Park Route 12 and drive 5.2 miles to a right turn on a dirt road immediately opposite the signed Desert Queen Mine Road, which heads south. Turn north on the one-lane dirt road and drive 1.4 miles to its end at the Pine City Backcountry Board and parking area. GPS: N34 1.413 / W116 4.658'

The Hike

This trip covers a variety of mine sites, from the most prosperous in the area (Desert Queen) to those that obviously were not successful. The Desert Queen was in operation from 1895 to 1961 and was one of the most productive gold mines in the Southern California desert. The magnitude of the Desert Queen operation is not evident from the gaping holes in the mountainside but from the massive tailings that drip like blood down the mountain into the wash below. The debris left around the site—which continues to appear miles down the wash—is also evidence of the environmental repercussions of the industrial use of the desert.

The experience of hiking down the wash erases the sight of the damage to the mountainside. The huge boulders that rise above and periodically in front of you, blocking your way, are reminders of the forces of nature that are still in operation. The vegetation of the wash is profuse and diverse. Mesquite, creosote, and smoke trees line the wash, sometimes even blocking your passage. The intermittent power of rushing water scours the wash, but these durable plants enjoy this location.

Mining sites farther down the wash represent the other end of the economic spectrum from the Desert Queen. Unlike the Keys operation, the other sites are small. The artifacts found around the miners' dwellings indicate a grim existence for these workers. This was primitive living. The size of the tailings shows that the excavations were not extensive. These mining projects did not last long.

Remains of a miner's bungalow at the Desert Queen Mine site.

Walking back up the wash after visiting John's Camp, you can revel in the beauties of the canyon. Then, turning the last corner, you encounter the mining equipment left in the wash by the Desert Queen. Two distinct worlds are preserved by Joshua Tree National Park; we can learn much by being aware of both of them.

Miles and Directions

0.0 From the trailhead, the broad trail goes east. Disregard the cable barricade, which was put there to deter vehicles, not hikers.

0.3 At the old stone ruins of a miner's dwelling, the rocky road winds down to the wash below.

0.6 Overlook. Climb to the mines, then return to the wash.

1.3 Huge boulders block the wash. Take the crude trail on the bank to the right (west) to get around these obstacles.

1.5 Where the wash widens, the old prospector site is on the low shelf to your right.

1.8 Another boulder tumble blocks the narrow wash. Follow the cairns and the game trail to the left.

2.0 At the silvery "anthill" above the wash on the left bank, bear right to the John's Camp site on the low bank on the right.

4.0 Return to the trailhead by walking back up the wash.

25 Pine City/Canyon

The short option on this hike takes you to a picturesque former mining camp. The longer, more adventurous outing heads on down the colorful canyon, with several steep rock pitches requiring some scrambling near the North Entrance, where your car shuttle awaits you.

Start: 15 miles south of Twentynine Palms.
Distance: 6.5 miles one way.
Approximate hiking time: 2 to 4 hours for short hike; 5 to 7 for longer one.
Difficulty: Easy (Pine City); strenuous (Pine City Canyon).

Trail surface: Clear trail to Pine City; cross-country on mostly clear washes down Pine City Canyon.
Seasons: October through May.
Maps: Trails Illustrated Joshua Tree National Park; USGS Queen Mountain.
Trail contact: Joshua Tree National Park (see appendix D).

Finding the trailhead: From the visitor center in Twentynine Palms, continue south on Utah Trail 8.2 miles to the Pinto Y intersection. Stay to the right on Park Route 12 for 5.1 miles to the unsigned dirt road on your right (directly opposite Desert Queen Mine Road, which goes south). Turn right (north) on the dirt road and drive 1.4 miles to the end of the road at the Pine City Backcountry Board. GPS: N34 1.41301.967' / W116 4.658'

For car shuttle: Park at the North Entrance introduction board, 0.5 mile south of the North Entrance on the west side of PR 12. The North Entrance is 4 miles south of Twentynine Palms. GPS: N34 4.446' / W116 1.923'

The Hike

Except for a few mine shafts grated over for public safety, all that remains of Pine City is the wind rustling through the pines. Still, the short and easy walk to the Pine City site provides ample opportunities for exploration and for savoring its bouldery beauty. The trail maintains an even grade across a high Mojave Desert plateau covered with Joshua trees.

At mile 1.1 an obscure trail leads to the right for 0.3 mile to a picture-perfect pocket of monzoquartz granite ringed with piñon pines. The main trail to Pine City continues left. At 1.6 miles another trail takes off to the right, dropping 100 feet in 0.2 mile to the dry Pine Spring. The spring lies just above the narrow notch of a steep, boulder-strewn canyon. This pleasant spot is well suited for a picnic or for just plain relaxing. Bighorn sheep rely on the cool shelter of this place when people aren't there.

Note: To avoid disturbance of sheep and other wildlife, the Pine City/Pine Spring/upper Pine Canyon area is within a much larger day-use area. Camping is currently allowed south of Pine City in accordance with park regulations. Check at the visitor center in case these boundaries are altered.

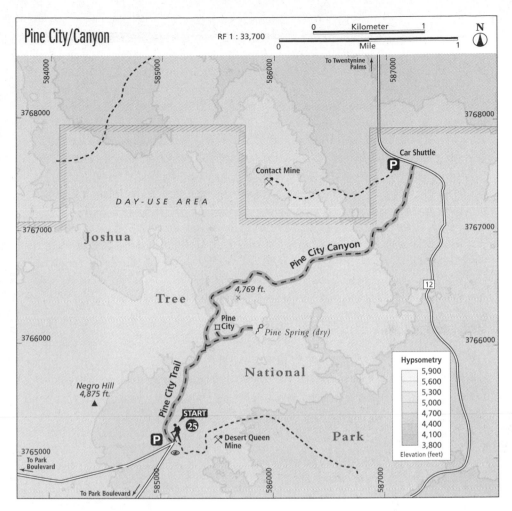

RF 1 : 33,700

Kilometer

Mile

N

To Twentynine
Palms

Car Shuttle

Contact Mine

DAY-USE AREA

Joshua

Pine City Canyon

4,769 ft.

Tree

Pine
City

Pine Spring (dry)

Pine City Trail

National

Negro Hill
4,875 ft.

START
25

Desert Queen
Mine

Park

To Park
Boulevard

To Park Boulevard

Hypsometry

	5,900
	5,600
	5,300
	5,000
	4,700
	4,400
	4,100
	3,800

Elevation (feet)

From the Pine Spring turnoff, continue left another 0.1 mile to the Pine City site, which is immediately east of the trail in a wide, sandy flat next to a huge round boulder sitting atop a rock platform. You could easily spend several hours poking around the myriad side canyons and interesting rock formations that surround the Pine City site. The site contains at least one grated mine shaft and at least one more that is unsecured, so caution is called for. Return the way you came to complete this level 3.4-mile out-and-back hike.

To continue a point-to-point trip down Pine City Canyon, stay left on the trail for another 0.5 mile northeast of the Pine City site, to where it ends on a ridge next to a small hill. Drop into the broad saddle southwest of the 4,769-foot hill shown on the topographic map. If time and energy permit, this hill provides an easy walkup for a stunning view in all directions. From the saddle, drop down the steep gully to the main Pine City Canyon wash. A few rock cairns mark the way.

Looking down lower Pine City Canyon.

The upper reaches of Pine City Canyon are spectacular, lined with great columns of gray and red rock. The canyon drops steeply, requiring boulder hopping and, at times, the use of "all fours" to negotiate the steep but stable rocks. For out-and-back hikers wishing to sample a bit of this steep-walled canyon, hike a mile or so down to about the 4,000-foot level to a good turnaround point. This upper stretch harbors the deepest and most dramatic section of the canyon. Below 4,000 feet the canyon narrows and steepens with several more difficult rock sections requiring skill and agility with both hands and feet. Here the canyon is trending east to northeast and is dropping about 500 feet per mile. Multicolored bands of rippled rock—purple, red, yellow—grace the floor of this canyon lined with barrel cacti.

At 3,350 feet the country begins to open up. Although high ridges are nearby, the wash leaves the deeper canyon. This is also where the transition from the high Mojave Desert to the lower Colorado Desert becomes apparent, where cholla cacti dot the open desert. The last 2 miles involve easy walking down a broad wash to PR 12, a mellow time to relax and reflect upon the rugged splendor of Pine City Canyon. The wash meets the highway about 0.2 mile south of the parking area/introduction board, which is 0.5 mile south of the North Entrance.

Miles and Directions

0.0 Start at the Pine City Backcountry Board/trailhead.

1.1 Continue left at the trail junction with the right-hand trail leading to an old mine site.

1.6 Continue left at the right-hand trail to Pine Spring.

1.7 Arrive at the Pine City site. Turn around here to return to the trailhead.

2.2 The trail ends on a ridge above Pine City Canyon.

2.3 The use trail drops to Pine City Canyon.

6.5 The Pine City Canyon wash meets PR 12.

26 Contact Mine

Just inside the North Entrance to the park lies this historic gold-and-silver mine. It's a steep rocky trail to the mine site, but you will be rewarded with a splendid view, as well as the opportunity to get a feel for life as a desert miner.

Start: 4.5 miles south of Twentynine Palms.
Distance: 3.4 miles out and back.
Approximate hiking time: 3 to 5 hours.
Difficulty: Strenuous.
Trail surface: Rocky path.

Seasons: October through April.
Maps: Trails Illustrated Joshua Tree National Park; USGS Queen Mountain.
Trail contact: Joshua Tree National Park (see appendix D).

The Contact Mine sits on the hillside above the trail.

Finding the trailhead: From California Highway 62 in Twentynine Palms, take Utah Trail south 4 miles to the North Entrance of the park; continue on Park Route 12 for 0.5 mile to the trailhead on the right (west), at the park-entrance information board and parking area. GPS: N34 4.446'/ W116 1.923'

The Hike

The old mining trail that takes you to the Contact Mine is as impressive in its engineering as the mine itself. The old road cuts through solid rock, avoids gullies with remarkable rock foundations, and cuts across the sides of steep hills. The hiking path has become very rocky due to erosion, but the workmanship of the original road builders is still evident.

The hiker is exposed to the elements along the entire trail. Pick a cool day to enjoy this one!

The rising trail provides stunning views into the Pinto Mountains to the east, as well as into the craggy chain of peaks running from Twentynine Palms southward. At each bend in the trail, as it winds around another rocky ridge, you expect to see the mine. Not until 1.6 miles are you rewarded with the sight of the mine above on the hillside. At this point are side trails developed by the miners to handle two-way traffic. Count on spending additional time at the mine to prowl around the buildings and other artifacts, but beware of unsecured and hazardous mine shafts.

The hike back down reinforces one's awe with the work involved with developing the Contact Mine in the early 1900s.

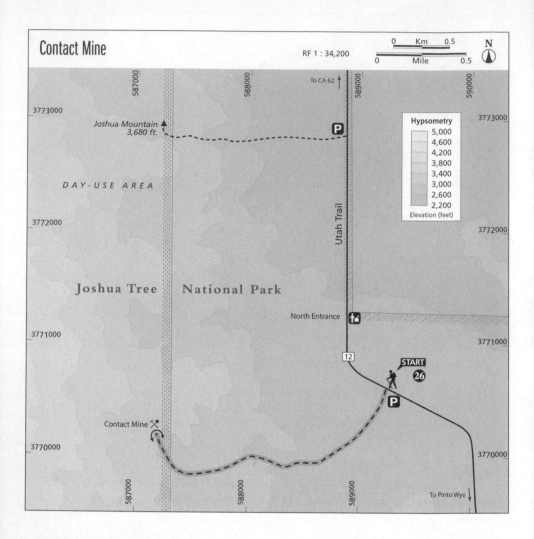

Contact Mine

RF 1 : 34,200

Miles and Directions:

0.0–0.2 From the board, follow the old jeep trail southwest and left of the huge boulders that stand apart from the other disorganized piles of granite.

0.2 At the wash, take the trail on top of the dike on the right.

0.4 At the dike's end, bear right, with the wash on a faint trail around a boulder pile.

0.45 There's a rising road ramp, dating from mining days, on the left across the wash. Take this ramp up from the wash and follow the road to the mine. Cairns mark the trail.

1.6 The mine site becomes visible on the mountainside above.

1.7 Arrive at the day-use-only mine site.

3.4 Return to the trailhead.

27 Fortynine Palms Oasis

This 3-mile round-trip hike rewards the energetic hiker with a display of fan palms and a lush willow thicket, a favorite habitat for birds and bighorn sheep. Visitors are asked to stay on the trail to minimize damage to the vegetation.

Start: 6 miles west of Twentynine Palms and 11 miles east of Joshua Tree.
Distance: 3 miles out and back.
Approximate hiking time: 2 to 4 hours.
Difficulty: Moderate.
Trail surface: Rocky path.

Seasons: October through April.
Maps: Trails Illustrated Joshua Tree National Park; USGS Queen Mountain.
Trail contact: Joshua Tree National Park (see appendix D).

Finding the trailhead: From California Highway 62, 11.2 miles east of Park Boulevard in Joshua Tree, take Fortynine Palms Canyon Road south to the end (2 miles). From Twentynine Palms, take CA 62 for 5.5 miles west of Twentynine Palms to the Fortynine Palms Canyon Road exit, then south 2 miles to the road's end at a parking area. GPS: N34 7.173 / W116 6.730'

The towering palms of Fortynine Palms Oasis.

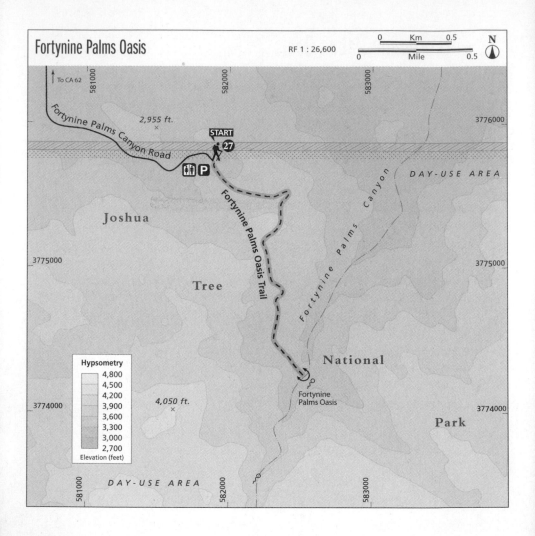

Fortynine Palms Oasis

RF 1 : 26,600

The Hike

This is a clear but rocky trail to the Fortynine Palms Oasis. From the parking lot, it climbs to its highest point in the first half of the trip; from this elevation you have a view of Twentynine Palms, and shortly later, as the trail curves to the right, you have your first glimpse of the palms 0.75 mile ahead, down in a rocky gorge. The descent to the oasis traverses dry, rocky terrain; even the desert shrubs are dwarfed by the harsh conditions. Miniature barrel cacti dot the slopes. The windy, dry hills above make the oasis even more striking.

At Fortynine Palms the huge old palms tower above a dense willow thicket that provides a congenial habitat for numerous desert birds. Hummingbirds are frequent visitors. The canyon is also a mecca for desert bighorn sheep. In this idyllic setting, the palm trees have a bizarre appearance. Their fire-scarred trunks bear tragic witness to the destructive urges of knife-wielding visitors who have tattooed the trunks with initials, signs, and names. The sight of these assaults on the palms is incongruous in such a setting, and highly disturbing.

Hikers should stay on the trail to avoid trampling young vegetation at the oasis. The multitude of use trails are damaging rare plants and endangering the next generation of palm trees.

For the adventuresome and energetic explorer, the canyon beyond the oasis (to the right) can be explored as far as time and interest permit. The use trail is intermittent, and the boulders are challenging, but the curving canyon is inviting. After your exploration, the hike back to the parking lot provides sweeping views of the desert below.

Note: Day use only is permitted in this area to protect bighorn-sheep access to the water supply.

Miles and Directions

0.0   From the parking area, hike up the trail on the slope south of the roadway.

0.3   The trail makes a sharp turn to the right; continue climbing.

0.5   Climb to the top of the ridge, where you'll have your first view of the oasis.

1.0   Cross the wash and continue downhill.

1.5   Arrive at the oasis, and explore the valley beyond if desired.

3.0   Return to the trailhead.

28 Sneakeye Spring

The climb to the dry spring involves scrambling over and around elephantine boulders, which clog the steep canyon. This is a hike for the hardy, with the reward of visiting a high hidden valley.

Start: 10 miles west of Twentynine Palms.
Distance: 1 mile out and back.
Approximate hiking time: 2 to 3 hours.
Difficulty: Strenuous, with boulder scrambling.
Trail surface: Dirt path to cross-country boulder route in canyon.

Seasons: October through April.
Maps: Trails Illustrated Joshua Tree National Park; USGS Indian Cove.
Trail contact: Joshua Tree National Park (see appendix D).

Finding the trailhead: From California Highway 62, 9.8 miles east of Park Boulevard in Joshua Tree, take Indian Cove Road south 3 miles to the campground. Bear right at the Y intersection and follow signs for the hiking trail parking area.

From Twentynine Palms, take CA 62 for 7 miles west of the Utah Trail junction to Indian Cove Road. Go south on Indian Cove 3 miles to the campground entrance. Bear right and follow signs to the hiking trail parking area. GPS: N34 5.681 / W116 10.111'

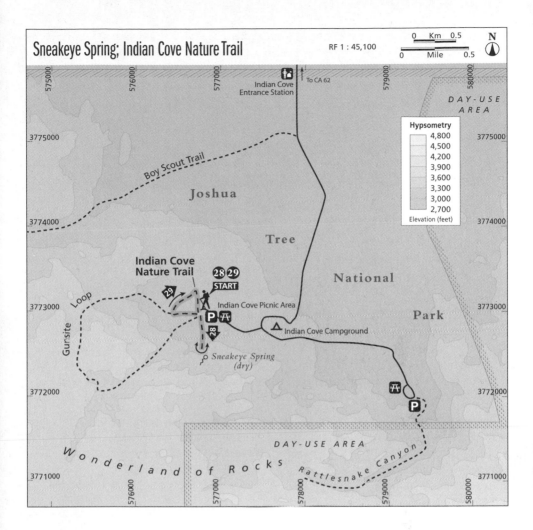

Sneakeye Spring; Indian Cove Nature Trail

RF 1 : 45,100

The Hike

This short but challenging hike takes you from a busy region of the park to an isolated high valley with pockets of greenery and oak trees, although the spring no longer is in evidence. This is a journey to an untrammeled wilderness. Due to its difficult entrance through the boulder-filled gorge, this hike appeals only to the adventuresome audience.

The first portion of the hike is deceptively easy. Curving around the monzogranite, the trail is clear and level. Only when you arrive at the wash will you perceive the difficulties that lie ahead. Careful climbing through the boulders is a pleasure due to their grainy surface. The greater hazard is the rapacious catclaw springing up wherever there is any earth available.

◀   *The rocky draw, filled with granite boulders, makes the Sneakeye Spring hike challenging.*

The high valley you reach on the northern edge of the Wonderland of Rocks has several side canyons to explore and mature oak trees for shade and relaxation. There is no water, in spite of the name of the hike; be sure to bring plenty with you.

Descending through the boulders can be as tricky as climbing them. The 1-mile distance of the hike is misleading because such boulder travel is very time-consuming.

Miles and Directions

0.0 From the parking area, follow the trail southwest around large boulders.

0.2 Drop into the wash. The easiest ascent of the canyon is via the sandy hill to the west (on the left).

0.3 At the top of the sandy slope, begin climbing over the elephantine boulders into the canyon.

0.5 There are several branches of canyon to explore from here.

1.0 Return to the parking area.

29 Indian Cove Nature Trail

Situated on the northern edge of the Wonderland of Rocks, this short nature trail at the Indian Cove Campground features information about desert-wash vegetation.

See map on page 83.
Start: 12 miles east of Joshua Tree and 10 miles west of Twentynine Palms.
Distance: 0.6-mile loop.
Approximate hiking time: Less than an hour.
Difficulty: Easy.

Trail surface: Sandy wash.
Seasons: October through April.
Maps: Trails Illustrated Joshua Tree National Park; USGS Indian Cove.
Trail contact: Joshua Tree National Park (see appendix D).

Finding the trailhead: From California Highway 62, 9.8 miles east of Park Boulevard in Joshua Tree, take Indian Cove Road south 3 miles to the campground. Bear right at the Y intersection and follow the signs for the nature trail parking area.

From the east, take CA 62 for 7 miles west of the Utah Trail intersection in Twentynine Palms; take Indian Cove Road south 3 miles to the campground and follow signs to the parking lot for the nature trail. GPS: N34 5.681 / W116 10.111'

The Hike

This self-guided nature trail is one of the more difficult such paths to follow due to scarcity of arrows, trail indicators, and informational signs. It begins just west of the parking area then travels across an alluvial fan and down into a broad wash. A short 0.2 mile later, it exits the wash and returns to the parking area.

The information provided ranges from background on Paleo-Indians to desert plant and animal identification to physical geology. There is no thematic common denominator.

It's easy to miss the path's exit from the wash. Watch for the desert senna identification sign on your right immediately after the paperbag bush sign. That's your signal to bear right out of the wash to pick up the trail back to the parking area.

30 Wall Street Mill

With a pretentious name to attract the big investors from the east, this site will be of interest to the mining historian. Artifacts of the ranching past are also plentiful near the Keys homestead. The adjacent Wonderland of Rocks provides contrast with these defunct desert enterprises.

Start: 20 miles southeast of the town of Joshua Tree.
Distance: 2 miles out and back.
Approximate hiking time: 2 to 4 hours.
Difficulty: Easy.
Trail surface: Dirt path.

Seasons: October through April.
Maps: Trails Illustrated Joshua Tree National Park; USGS Indian Cove.
Trail contact: Joshua Tree National Park (see appendix D).

The rusty remains of the Wall Street Mill sit atop the hill adjacent to the majestic Wonderland of Rocks.

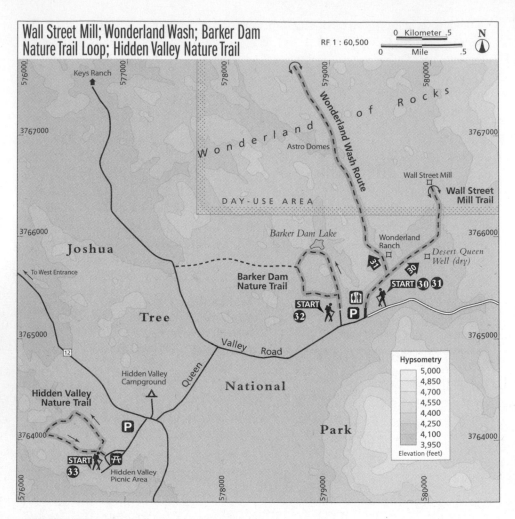

RF 1 : 60,500

Finding the trailhead: From California Highway 62 in Joshua Tree, take the Park Boulevard exit and go 1 mile south to where it becomes Quail Springs Road; continue on Quail Springs Road 4 miles to the park's West Entrance. Follow Park Route 12 for 8.7 miles to Hidden Valley Campground/Barker Dam Road. Turn left (east) into the campground. Bear right immediately after the entrance and follow the paved road 1.6 miles to the Barker Dam Road and parking area. GPS: N34 1.363 / W116 9.394'

The Hike

From the common trailhead, follow the park sign to the right for the Wall Street Mill. This level hike displays the desert's power of preservation. Rusty old trucks still have their tires. Antique cars sit peacefully beneath oak trees. The mill, protected by the National Register of Historic Places due to its local technological and mechanical uniqueness, still stands with its machinery intact, albeit a tad rusty. A barbed-wire fence also protects the mill from visitors. Nearby are hulks of vehicles and other artifacts of life in the desert seventy or so years ago. A park sign at the mill explains its workings, with an excellent drawing—actually a blueprint of its original design in the 1920s. This is a fun voyage of discovery, even for those who might not be machinery buffs.

The ranch house to the left of the trail and the windmill at mile 0.5 are remnants of the ranching era in the Queen Valley. The Keys family has been involved in both ranching and mining for the past century.

The Wall Street Mill was part of the Keys's industrial complex. Built by Bill Keys to process the ore from the Desert Queen Mine, it was in operation for only a few years before falling into disuse. One reason for its short life span is that Bill Keys had a run-in with Worth Bagley, his neighbor, over the use of the road to the mill. The painted rock at 0.7 mile marks the spot of the final altercation and of Bagley's death. Convicted of murder, Keys spent five years in prison but was later exonerated. Apparently he had shot Bagley in self-defense.

The trail shares its trailhead with the Wonderland Wash hike. The proximity of the mill and the mounds of monzogranite provide appropriate contrast between the reign of man and of nature in this wild country.

Return to the parking area by the same dirt path.

Miles and Directions

0.0 From the Barker Dam parking area, take the Wall Street Mill trail to the east.

0.2 At the former parking area for the mill and Wonderland Wash, continue east.

0.3 Turn right at the fork. The ruins of a pink adobe house are 200 yards to your left.

0.4 Two paths come together: If you were tempted to visit the ruins, this is where you will rejoin the mill route.

0.5 With the windmill and debris on your right, continue north, parallel to Wonderland Wash.

0.7 Observe the modern petroglyph commemorating the death of Worth Bagley, for which Bill Keys served time in San Quentin.

1.0 Arrive at the mill site. After exploring the various artifacts, return to the trailhead via the same route.

2.0 Arrive at the trailhead.

31 Wonderland Wash

This flat, easy hike leads into the Wonderland of Rocks, a fantasyland of monzo-granite sculptures and mounds. You will probably have lots of company, for this is a favorite location for Joshua Tree rock climbers.

See map on page 86.
Start: 20 miles southeast of the town of Joshua Tree.
Distance: 2 miles out and back (longer for exploration).
Approximate hiking time: 1 to 3 hours.
Difficulty: Easy.

Trail surface: Sandy path.
Seasons: October through April.
Maps: Trails Illustrated Joshua Tree National Park; USGS Indian Cove.
Trail contact: Joshua Tree National Park (see appendix D).

Finding the trailhead: From California Highway 62 in the town of Joshua Tree, take Park Boulevard south 1 mile to where it becomes Quail Springs Road. Continue on Quail Springs Road 4 miles to the West Entrance of the park. Continue southeast on Park Route 12 for 8.7 miles to the Hidden Valley Campground. Turn left into the campground and take the immediate right turn (signed to Barker Dam). Follow this paved road 1.6 miles to the first road on your left, which goes to the parking area. GPS: N34°01.49940' / W116°08.50260'

The trail up Wonderland Wash winds through myriad granite boulders of all sizes.

The Hike

The use trail into Wonderland Wash is easy to follow due to the footsteps of the hundreds of rock climbers who enjoy these acres of White Tank granite. From the parking area, follow the signed trail to the east to the first fork, and bear left toward the ruins of a pink house, which you can see from the fork. Head for the house, then follow the beaten path to the left into the nearby shallow wash, only about 50 feet from the house site. The narrow wash is easy to follow, with periodic pathways weaving from bank to bank as you follow it northward into the Wonderland.

Plentiful oak and prickly pear, as well as the remnants of a dam in the wash, are other attractions of this hike—but the primary focus is on the huge rock formations that stretch in all directions. This is an enchanted world of whimsically eroded granite mounds. Well into the wash (1 mile from the trailhead) are the formations known as the Astro Domes to rock climbers who enjoy scaling their massive surfaces. The voices of climbers usually can be heard echoing from various points among the boulders, and their silhouettes may startle you when they appear hundreds of feet above atop these obelisks.

The trip back down the wash to the trailhead will be equally interesting, because the rock formations look different from the new angle.

Miles and Directions

0.0 From the parking area, take the signed trail heading east. At the first fork, bear left to the ruins of a pink adobe ranch house.

0.5 Cut by the house and enter the wash to your left, following the beaten use trail.

0.6 Continue winding north in the wash, between awesome rock formations.

1.0 The huge domes of monzogranite are the Astro Domes.

2.0 Return to the parking area.

32 Barker Dam Nature Trail Loop

A 1.1-mile loop, this trail has something to appeal to every hiker: spectacular geology, the only lake in the park, a rich array of petroglyphs, artifacts of the ranching era, and information about desert plant life and its uses by Native Americans.

See map on page 86.
Start: 20 miles southeast of the town of Joshua Tree.
Distance: 1.1-mile loop.
Approximate hiking time: 1 to 2 hours.
Difficulty: Easy.

Trail surface: Sandy path.
Seasons: October through April.
Maps: Trails Illustrated Joshua Tree National Park; USGS Indian Cove.
Trail contact: Joshua Tree National Park (see appendix D).

Finding the trailhead: From California Highway 62 in Joshua Tree, take Park Boulevard south 1 mile to where it turns into Quail Springs Road; continue on Quail Springs Road 4 miles to the West Entrance of the park. Follow Park Route 12 for 8.7 miles to the Hidden Valley Campground and Barker Dam turnoff to the left (east); bear right at the paved road immediately after entering the campground and drive 1.6 miles to the Barker Dam Road parking lot. GPS: N34 1.36301.153' / W116 9.394'

The Hike

This highly informative nature trail is a step back in time, both in terms of prehistory and with respect to the futile, short-lived attempts to raise cattle back in the early 1900s. Barker Dam was built by ranchers Barker and Shay in a natural rock catch basin to store water for cattle. In 1949–1950 the dam was raised by Bill Keys, owner of the Desert Queen Mine and the nearby Keys Ranch, then a private inholding. When filled to capacity by seasonal rains, the lake behind the dam encompasses twenty acres. Because it is surrounded by a magnificent rock ring of monzonite granite, it looks almost as though it is nestled in a high Sierra cirque at 11,000 feet. Today, the lake is used by bighorn sheep and many other species of wildlife, including shorebirds and migratory waterfowl—some of the last creatures one would expect to find in the desert!

The trail is clear and sandy, winding through a couple of tight places in the rocks, reaching Barker Dam at 0.4 mile. Notable plant species en route include Turbinella oak, adapted to the high Mojave Desert above 4,000 feet, and nolina, a yucca lookalike that provided food for the Cahuilla Indians, who baked it like molasses.

Bill Keys built innovative stone watering basins, designed to prevent spillage of the precious desert water, below the dam.

From Barker Dam Lake the trail heads west and south through a series of intimate little alcovelike valleys containing rock-lined gardens of Joshua trees, cholla, and yucca. At 0.8 mile the trail comes to a signed path leading 100 feet right to a large panel of petroglyphs, which are etchings in stone made by early Native Americans. The petroglyphs are on the face of a large rock amphitheater/overhang. Sadly, a movie crew painted the carvings so that they would show up better on film. The rock faces just to the southeast of these vandalized petroglyphs contain undamaged petroglyphs, which are largely concealed by dense brush. This early encampment of immeasurable value includes rock mortars used for the grinding of nuts and seeds along with petroglyphs of a scorpion, a man with long fingers, women in dresses, who were likely early settlers, and other figures better left to your imagination. Vegetation is being re-established along this cliff wall, so please be careful to avoid trampling the new plantings and other vegetation.

The loop continues another 0.3 mile back to the parking area/trailhead.

◀ *Barker Dam was built at a narrow spot in the canyon.*

Miles and Directions

0.0 Start from the Barker Dam parking area.

0.4 Arrive at Barker Dam Lake.

0.8 Take the signed path that leads to a large panel of petroglyphs.

1.1 The loop ends back at the parking lot.

33 Hidden Valley Nature Trail

Ringed by mounds of monzogranite boulders, this is truly a hidden valley. The nature trail winds around the valley, with signs about local history and desert ecology. You may be distracted, however, by the sight of the rock climbers scrambling and swinging overhead.

See map on page 86.
Start: 14 miles southeast of the town of Joshua Tree.
Distance: 1-mile loop.
Approximate hiking time: 1 to 2 hours.
Difficulty: Easy.

Trail surface: Sandy path.
Seasons: October through April.
Maps: Trails Illustrated Joshua Tree National Park; USGS Indian Cove.
Trail contact: Joshua Tree National Park (see appendix D).

Finding the trailhead: From California Highway 62 at Joshua Tree, take Park Boulevard south 1 mile to where it becomes Quail Springs Road. Continue on Quail Springs Road 4 miles to the West Entrance of the park; stay on the same road (now Park Route 12) 8.7 miles to the Hidden Valley Nature Trail and Picnic Area on your right. After you turn off the main road, follow the paved road to the right less than 0.1 mile to the parking area. GPS: N34 0.724 / W116 10.083'

The Hike

The trail from the parking area winds upward through the boulders to Hidden Valley. This part of the trail consists of old asphalt, so following it is easy. The rest of the journey is unpaved but clearly marked with signs, arrows, or fallen logs. There is some low-intensity rock walking.

Many possible pathways diverge in all directions within the valley. Most are created by the numerous adventuresome rock climbers who are attracted to the massive blocks of granite that create the valley walls. It is likely that you will hear and see them on your hike.

New signs along the nature trail emphasize natural history, sustainability in the desert, and human activities. The abnormally high rainfall (10 inches per year) of the late nineteenth century led to the development of cattle ranches here. The McHaney Gang allegedly used Hidden Valley as a base camp for their large rustling operation in the Southwest until they turned their energies to gold mining. They began developing the

The monzogranite boulders of Hidden Valley attract rock climbers.

Desert Queen Mine in 1895. It was eventually taken over by Bill Keys, who became quite the desert magnate—a successful rancher and miner until his death in 1969.

The advent of the automobile in the 1920s brought new visitors aplenty to the desert, seriously endangering the fragile environment. In the 1930s Minerva Hamilton Hoyt led efforts to protect the region, resulting finally in Franklin D. Roosevelt's 1936 declaration of Joshua Tree National Monument. In 1950 the boundary of the monument was sizably reduced in order to permit extensive mining. The larger area was restored with the California Desert Protection Act of 1994.

Note: This is a day-use area; no camping is permitted.

34 Boy Scout Trail/Willow Hole

This hike skirts along the western edge of the Wonderland of Rocks, with an out-and-back trip to Willow Hole, deep within the Wonderland, ending at Indian Cove Road.

Start: 11.4 miles southeast of the town of Joshua Tree.
Distance: 12 miles one way.
Approximate hiking time: 6 to 10 hours.
Difficulty: Moderate (for south to north downhill); strenuous (from north to south uphill).
Trail surface: Clear trail/wash with a steep but good trail segment between miles 4 and 5.

Seasons: October through April (Boy Scout Trail); October through May (Willow Hole).
Maps: Trails Illustrated Joshua Tree National Park; USGS Indian Cove.
Trail contact: Joshua Tree National Park (see appendix D).

The path is fairly level near the south end of the Boy Scout Trail.

Finding the trailhead: From California Highway 62 at Joshua Tree, take Park Boulevard south 1 mile to where it becomes Quail Springs Road; follow it another 4 miles to the West Entrance of the park. Continue 6.9 miles to the Keys West Backcountry Board, which is the starting trailhead, on the left (north) side of the highway.

    Car shuttle: From CA 62, 9.8 miles east of Park Boulevard, take Indian Cove Road south 1.6 miles to the Indian Cove Backcountry Board on your right (west side of the road). GPS: N34°06.78720' / W116°09.32280'

The Hike

The Boy Scout Trail provides access to several high-quality hikes within and adjacent to the Wonderland of Rocks. The most complete and enjoyable choice is to hike mostly downhill from the Keys West Backcountry Board to the Indian Cove Backcountry Board, taking in an excursion deep into the fascinating Wonderland of Rocks at Willow Hole. This 12-mile journey on foot samples much of the diversity of this amazing landscape. If a car shuttle is out of the question, an excellent second choice is to hike 6.6 miles out and back to Willow Hole. This trip shares the first 1.3 miles of the Boy Scout Trail from the Keys West Backcountry Board.

    The popular, well-signed Boy Scout Trail climbs gradually along the west side of the Wonderland of Rocks through a picturesque Joshua tree forest sprinkled with yucca and cholla cacti, gaining only 90 feet in the first 1.3 miles. The trail offers gorgeous views of the San Bernardino Mountains to the southwest, and the nearby mounds of monzonite quartz add a real sense of majesty to this high Mojave Desert country. The right side (east) of the entire Boy Scout Trail is open to day use only so that desert wildlife can visit water sources undisturbed. Backpackers can camp on the west side as long as they are at least 500 feet from the trail. Also, be advised that there is no public access to the Keys Ranch inholding, which is just east of the Boy Scout Trail during the first 0.5 mile.

The following two legs of the hike are described from the trail junction at 1.3 miles. The right-hand trail leads to Willow Hole and is signed DAY USE ONLY. The left fork is the Boy Scout Trail and is signed HORSE AND FOOT TRAIL AND INDIAN COVE 7 MILES.

Willow Hole

The clear, sandy trail maintains a fairly constant but gradual downhill grade in a northeasterly direction, winding through impressive columns and pillars of White Tank granite. At 2.5 miles the trail enters and follows a sandy wash. At 2.7 miles a wash enters from the right; continue left down the wider wash. At 3 miles another wash joins from the right, which makes for a tempting side trip into a secluded little valley. A large boulder blocks the wash 0.2 mile up, which is a good turnaround point; or you can continue up a bit farther by lifting yourself up and through the narrow rock notch to the clear wash beyond. Double-back to the Willow Hole wash. At 3.1 miles the wash widens into a huge circular bowl surrounded by majestic cliffs. Willow Hole comes into view at 3.3 miles with its dense tangle of large willow trees creating a moist microenvironment that holds seasonal pools of water. To get to the other side of the grove, bend down and walk through the center of Willow Hole on an overgrown use trail or take a well-worn use trail around the right side. Either way the view from the east end of Willow Hole is very worthwhile, especially down the wash toward Rattlesnake Canyon. Retrace your route 2 miles back to the trail junction, now at 5.3 miles total. At about 3.9 miles on the way back, it is possible to take the wrong wash in a narrow, rocky area. In general, stay right on the more traveled wash.

Boy Scout Trail

From the trail junction at 5.3 miles, take the right-hand fork, which is signed HORSE AND FOOT TRAIL AND INDIAN COVE 7 MILES. For the next 2 miles, the trail stays fairly level in a high Joshua tree plateau with yucca/rock gardens galore. After climbing at mile 7, the trail gradually drops along rocky side gullies but remains clear and easy to follow. At about 7.5 miles until the end, the trail is occasionally marked with steel pipe with two white stripes on top along with a few wooden posts. At 7.6 miles the trail drops into and follows a clear wash to mile 8, where a cement water trough and constructed rock wall are found in the wash.

At 8.2 miles the trail leaves the wash, making a sharp turn to the left (west). This turn is easy to miss, so watch for a steel-pipe trail marker behind a piñon pine to the left. This is also where the wash narrows and drops steeply into an extremely rugged

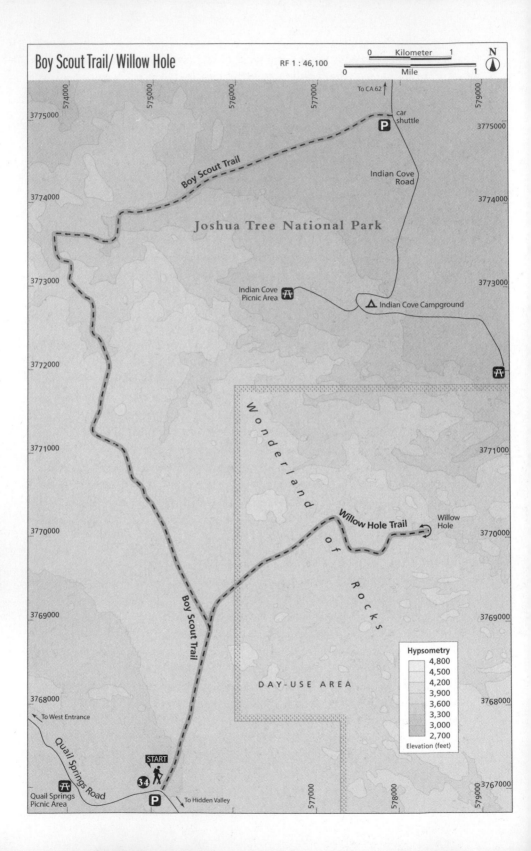

Boy Scout Trail/ Willow Hole

RF 1 : 46,100

0   Kilometer   1

0   Mile   1

N

To CA 62

car
shuttle

Indian Cove
Road

Boy Scout Trail

Joshua Tree National Park

Indian Cove
Picnic Area

Indian Cove Campground

W o n d e r l a n d

Willow Hole Trail

Willow
Hole

o f

R o c k s

Boy Scout Trail

DAY-USE AREA

Hypsometry

4,800
4,500
4,200
3,900
3,600
3,300
3,000
2,700

Elevation (feet)

To West Entrance

Quail Springs Road

Quail Springs
Picnic Area

START

34

To Hidden Valley

canyon. This constructed portion of the trail is narrow and rocky but in good condition. It drops and then climbs to mile 8.6, where a good view opens up to the canyon far below. The trail then switchbacks steeply down to a wash at mile 9; following the wash for another mile. The wash is easy walking but is bound by extremely steep rocky slopes and cliff rock near mile 10.

At mile 10 a steel pipe on the right marks the departure of the trail from the wash, where it then crosses over into the main wash, following it to mile 10.5. At mile 10.5 a well-marked trail climbs out of the wash to the right and cuts across 1.5 miles of open desert alluvial fan vegetated with creosote, yucca, cholla cacti, and Mormon tea. Most impressive are the recurring mounds of granite sprinkled like great dollops of frozen yogurt across the desert. At mile 12 the trail ends at the Indian Cove Backcountry Board.

Miles and Directions

0.0 Start from the Keys West Backcountry Board.

1.3 Arrive at the Boy Scout Trail/Willow Hole Trail junction. Follow the right-hand trail to Willow Hole.

2.5 The trail enters and follows a wash.

3.3 Arrive at Willow Hole. Retrace your steps back to the junction.

5.3 Reach the junction. Take the Boy Scout Trail to the right.

7.0 This is the high point of the trail at 4,250 feet.

7.6 The trail drops into and follows a wash.

8.0 A cement water trough and constructed rock wall are found in the wash.

8.2 The trail makes a sharp left turn out of the wash.

8.6 The rocky trail climbs to 4,070 feet for a panoramic view.

8.9 The trail drops into the wash and follows it for 1 mile.

10.0 Here the trail crosses over into a side gully, dropping to the main wash.

10.5 The trail leaves the canyon and cuts across open desert.

12.0 The trail ends at the Indian Cove Backcountry Board, where you pick up your car shuttle.

Options: For a three- to five-hour out-and-back hike, hike the 6.6 miles to Willow Hole. When you return to the trail junction at mile 5.3, take the left-hand trail back to the Keys West Backcountry Board. Another option is to skip Willow Hole and hike 8 miles directly to Indian Cove.

35 Quail Wash to West Entrance Wash

This point-to-point trip requires a car shuttle, but it is well worth the inconvenience. Along the way you will see dense stands of Joshua trees, historic cabin ruins, and a mine, and you'll have expansive views of Quail Mountain and several scenic side canyons to explore.

Start: 10 miles southeast of the town of Joshua Tree.
Distance: 8.2 miles one way (with car shuttle).
Approximate hiking time: 6 to 8 hours.
Difficulty: Moderate.
Trail surface: Dirt trail, sandy washes.

Seasons: October through May.
Maps: Trails Illustrated Joshua Tree National Park; USGS Joshua Tree South and Indian Cove.
Trail contact: Joshua Tree National Park (see appendix D).

Finding the trailhead: From California Highway 62 in the town of Joshua Tree, take Park Boulevard south 1 mile to where it becomes Quail Springs Road; continue 4 miles to the West Entrance. Continue 6.1 miles on Park Route 12 to Quail Springs Picnic Area on your right. GPS: N34°02.39580' / W116°11.80380'

Car shuttle: 1.2 miles inside of the West Entrance on PR 12 is a pullout on the north side of the road near the wash exit of the trail. The exit point of the hike is 1 mile south of the West Entrance on PR 12. GPS: N34°04.88760' / W116°15.08280'

The Hike

This hike requires skills in backcountry navigation. The trail starts out through an open Joshua tree desert ringed by a distant horizon of jagged peaks dotted with mounds of granite. The clear, sandy trail leads west-northwest and is easy to follow. At 0.6 mile it crosses the wash and continues on the left side, providing much firmer walking than the wash.

The trail angles closer to the rocky hillside on the left (south) and intersects the Johnny Lang Canyon trail at mile 2. This is the first major canyon to the south and makes for a strenuous but exciting option (see below). For this hike, continue west on the main trail after passing Johnny Lang Canyon. At mile 3 the trail passes by the second major canyon to the south, which leads up toward the highest point in the park: 5,813-foot Quail Mountain. At 3.2 miles several steel posts mark a fence line across the wash. The trail begins to leave the open desert, dropping into a wide gap through the mountains. At mile 4 the trail dips to the southwest and crosses the Smith Water Canyon Wash at 4.5 miles. Joshua trees are especially thick in this area. If time permits, this is an interesting place to explore, both in lower Smith Water Canyon and south toward the Quail Springs site shown on the topo map.

The open shaft at the Johnny Lang Mine. ▶

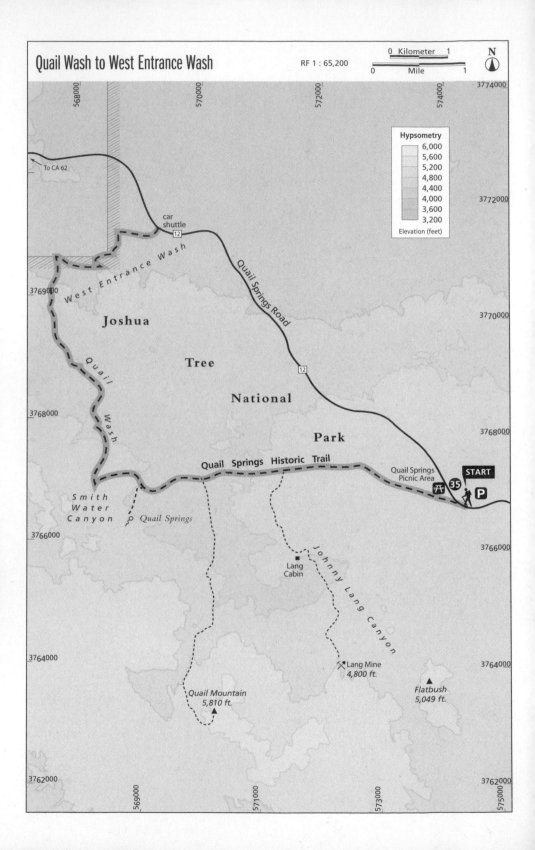

Quail Wash to West Entrance Wash

RF 1 : 65,200

Hypsometry

6,000
5,600
5,200
4,800
4,400
4,000
3,600
3,200

Elevation (feet)

N

0   Kilometer   1
0   Mile   1

To CA 62

car shuttle

12

West Entrance Wash

Quail Springs Road

Joshua

Tree

National

Park

Quail Wash

12

Quail Springs Historic Trail

Quail Springs Picnic Area

START

35

P

Smith Water Canyon

Quail Springs

Lang Cabin

Johnny Lang Canyon

Lang Mine
4,800 ft.

Flatbush
5,049 ft.

Quail Mountain
5,810 ft.

568000
570000
572000
574000

3774000
3772000
3770000
3768000
3766000
3764000
3762000

569000
571000
573000
575000

3769000
3768000
3766000
3764000
3762000

At 5 miles the trail/wash enters a recent burned-over area with fire-blackened Joshua trees dominating the landscape to the south. For the next 1.5 miles, the trail weaves in and out of the wash. For the most part the wash is easier to find and follow than the trail. At 6.5 miles the trail joins the wash at a National Park Service boundary fence in another burn area. At 6.7 miles the trail reaches a rock-cable boundary fence, which is signed NPS BOUNDARY US. Do not cross the fence onto the adjacent private property. Instead, turn right and follow the fence on a well-defined use trail eastward. Soon the trail disappears in West Entrance Wash. Continue up the wide sandy wash for about a mile. Look for a side wash angling left (northeast) next to a distinctive rock mound on the left. Head up this wash, where you'll come to a rock ledge dropoff within 0.1 mile. Climb up the ledge and continue up the wash another 0.4 mile to PR 12. At this point you've walked a good distance, so let's hope your shuttle will be waiting for you. If not, at least you're only a mile south of the West Entrance.

Miles and Directions

0.0 Start at the Quail Springs Picnic Area.

2.0 Arrive at the junction with the trail heading south up Johnny Lang Canyon. Stay to the right.

3.0 The trail passes the second major valley to the south, which leads toward Quail Mountain (5,813 feet).

4.5 The trail passes the mouth of Smith Water Canyon.

5.0 The trail enters a fire area.

6.7 The trail reaches the north boundary of the park; turn right (west) up West Entrance Wash.

7.7 Leave the West Entrance Wash and head northeast up a side wash.

8.2 Arrive at PR 12, 1 mile south of the West Entrance.

Option: This 6-mile out and back up Johnny Lang Canyon to the Lang Mine adds two to three hours to the Quail Wash hike. It's a strenuous side trip. The Lang Canyon trail intersects the Quail Springs Trail at mile 2. This is the first major canyon to the south. This trail is easy to miss, but it takes off from the main trail at a forty-five-degree angle heading southwest from near the foot of the ridge. The Johnny Lang Canyon trail passes just to the left of a small hill 0.2 mile up. It then crosses a wash at 0.3 mile, angling southwest to the base of the hill. It turns south for another mile to the Lang cabin site, staying on the right side of this wide lower valley all the way to the cabin ruins. If in doubt, follow the main Johnny Lang wash.

The remnants of the cabin, such as they are, are located on a bench about 50 feet to the right of the wash at 3,980 feet. All that remains are part of a rock foundation and piles of rusted cans and metal. A fairly well-defined use trail takes off from the cabin site. From here it is possible to see a large dark-topped hill (Point 4549 on the topo map) about 1 mile south; this is on the route leading up to the mine.

The use trail crosses the wash several times during the next 0.6 mile before coming to a manzanita flat just before a gully on the right. Cross the gully and head to the right up the ridge (south) toward the dark-topped hill (which has a knob and saddle to its left). On the backside of the hill, you'll intersect the rocky remains of an overgrown road that leads south into a gully below the mine. From this point you can see the mine tailings to the south, high on the hillside just below a prominent rock outcropping. Drop into the gully, then ascend the ridge southward, gaining 300 feet in the remaining 0.25 mile to the unsecured mine shaft. At 700 feet above the canyon, the mine entrance and platform is certainly a room with a view. Retrace your route for the 3-mile descent back to Quail Wash.

36 California Riding and Hiking Trail: Covington Flat to Keys View, Quail Mountain

On this trip lies the park's highest peak. It's a point-to-point hike, requiring a car shuttle, along a well-marked trail. The outing to the peak is a strenuous cross-country scramble, rewarded with outstanding views of the region.

Start: 12 miles south of the town of Joshua Tree.
Distance: 15 miles one way.
Approximate hiking time: 7 to 11 hours.
Difficulty: Moderate (R & H Trail); strenuous (Quail Mountain).
Trail surface: Dirt path; short cross-country section to peak.

Seasons: October through May.
Maps: Trails Illustrated Joshua Tree National Park; USGS Joshua Tree South; East Deception Canyon; and Keys View.
Trail contact: Joshua Tree National Park (see appendix D).

Finding the trailhead: From California Highway 62 and Park Boulevard in the town of Joshua Tree, go east on CA 62 for 3.4 miles to La Contenta. Turn right (south) on La Contenta and go 2.9 miles to Covington Flat Road. La Contenta is paved for only a mile; thereafter it is a washboardy narrow dirt road but suitable for passenger vehicles. Turn right at the backcountry trailhead sign and take a cut-over 1.9 miles to Upper Covington Flat Road. Turn left, again following signs to the Upper Covington Backcountry Board, on Upper Covington Flat Road and go 2 miles southeast to the board and parking area. The trail leaves from behind the board. GPS: N34°00.58800' / W116°18.32100'

If covering the continuous length of the California Riding and Hiking Trail is not your goal, this segment of the trail can also be accessed by continuing on the Lower Covington Flat Road to the dead end at the picnic area. The trail from the picnic area joins this trail after the first mile. GPS: N34°01.43760' / W116°17.86260'

Car shuttle: From CA 62 in Joshua Tree, take Park Boulevard south 1 mile to where it becomes Quail Springs Road, which you take for 4 miles to the West Entrance. Continue 10 miles on Park Route 12 to the intersection with Keys View Road (Park Route 13). Bear right on Keys View and drive 1 mile to the Juniper Flats Backcountry Board, near where the California Riding and Hiking Trail crosses Keys View Road. GPS: N33°58.67340' / W116°09.89040'

Polly Cunningham pauses at the 6-foot cairn on the windswept top of Quail Mountain.

The Hike

Neither wide nor well-pruned, this section of the California Riding and Hiking Trail is evidently not heavily traveled, although it is frequently signed with arrows and mileposts. This is definitely a long-pants excursion, or your legs will suffer on both the basic trail and the side trip to Quail Mountain.

Evidence of wildlife is considerably more plentiful on the first 5 miles of the trail from Covington Flat—deer, sheep, rabbits, rodents, coyotes—than elsewhere on the trail. Unlike the Riding and Hiking Trail segment out of the Black Rock Campground, this section shows no signs of use by horses. The first 5 miles are also highly enjoyable as you climb up and down over a series of descending ridges. The crest of each ridge provides a "Wow!" reaction as the panoramas of the park open before you. Even without climbing Quail Mountain, this section of the Riding and Hiking Trail provides sweeping vistas of the Little San Bernardino Range to the south, the Pinto Range to the east, and the various pinnacles in the central section of the park.

The climb to Quail Mountain is easy to plan from this south approach because the peak is visible from your takeoff point at milepost 23 on the Riding and Hiking Trail and most of the way after that as well. The approach up the wash is challenging, but it is better than trying the southeast ridge. The downfall of piñon limbs that makes the wash/ravine so difficult is the result of a 1978 burn on the mountain.

As you climb to the naked summit, you will be stunned by the dimensions of the cairn. It is a tower of well-placed rocks at least 5 feet high. From a distance,

California Riding and Hiking Trail: Covington Flat to Keys View, Quail Mountain

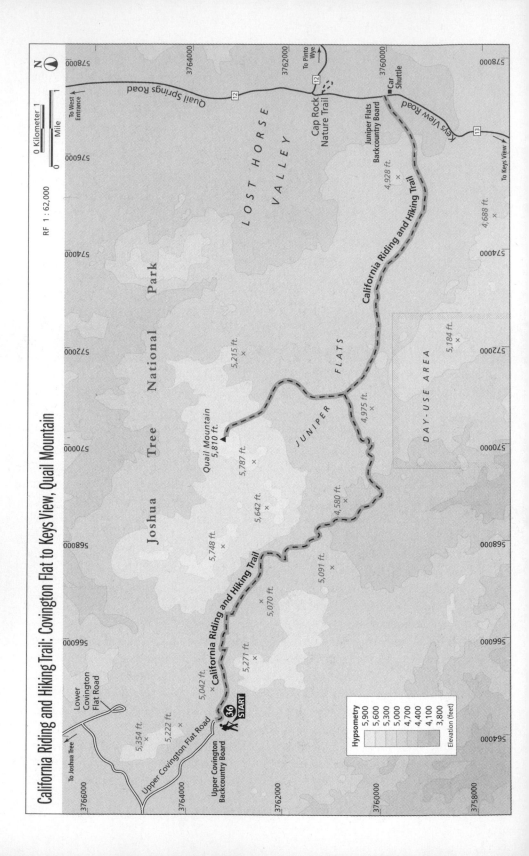

the mountain looks exactly like the bird for which it was named. The views from Quail Mountain are spectacular. The entire park spreads out in every direction. After enjoying the windy view, return via your route to the spur road and the Riding and Hiking Trail. The points you picked on your way up should help you locate the trail.

The last 5 miles down the Riding and Hiking Trail after the peak ascent are not anticlimactic. The overwhelming natural wonders of Joshua Tree are ever-present. The Wonderland of Rocks grows immense as you get farther into Juniper Flats. The White Tank formations of Ryan Mountain also become more massive as you approach Keys View Road. This hike represents the pinnacle of a Joshua Tree experience for both the ascent to the highest peak in the park and the journey through its wild heartland.

Miles and Directions

0.0–1.5 From the parking area, the well-marked trail goes over a ridge and along a hillside piñon-juniper forest. The largest Joshua tree is in 0.1 mile.

1.7 Bear right at the intersection with the spur trail from Covington Picnic Area at milepost 28.

2.0–3.5 The trail goes over a series of ridges.

5.0 Milepost 23, nearly hidden by a large juniper on your right, is the start point for a side trip to Quail Mountain. The road appears to be a flat wash lacking telltale wheel tracks. Turn left.

5.5 The road ends. Head northeast toward Quail Mountain. Look back and select distinctive features in the landscape to help you locate your return route. Cross through the prickly shrubbery toward a fire break that cuts over the northeast ridge.

6.1 You'll see two lower ridges and a wash—turn left and follow the wash toward the mountain. Note your location so you can exit here on your return trip.

6.4 Bear right at the fork in the wash after a rock outcropping of contorted striped strata on the left (west) side. (Cairns and footprints help.)

6.8 The wash becomes narrow, rocky, and littered with downed trees, but stay in the ravine.

7.1 Emerge from the ravine, which has finally petered out; scramble up to the ridge to the right.

7.5 A huge cairn marks the summit. Return the way you came.

10.0 Resume the trip to Keys View Road.

15.0 Arrive at the backcountry board, to the right of the trail.

37 Black Rock Loop Trail: Eureka Peak and Back via California Riding and Hiking Trail

From the backcountry board just south of the subdivisions of Yucca Valley, you can embark on a long hike to the highest summit in this section of the park. The route up is woodsy and primitive. On the loop trail down from the peak, it is not unusual to encounter equestrian traffic—and the horses have the right of way.

Start: 3 miles south of Yucca Valley.
Distance: 10.5-mile loop.
Approximate hiking time: 4 to 6 hours.
Difficulty: Strenuous.
Trail surface: Sandy wash and trail; road.
Seasons: October through May.

Maps: Trails Illustrated Joshua Tree National Park; USGS Yucca Valley South and Joshua Tree South.
Trail contact: Joshua Tree National Park (see appendix D).

Finding the trailhead: From California Highway 62 in Yucca Valley, turn south on Avalon Avenue. Go 0.7 mile to where it becomes Palomar Drive. Continue south on Palomar Drive for 2.3 miles to the left turn onto Joshua Tree Lane. Take Joshua Tree Lane for 1 mile to the dead end at San Marino Avenue, where you turn right. Continue on San Marino for 0.3 mile to its dead end at Black Rock Road. Turn left on Black Rock to the park entrance. The backcountry board, which looks unlike all other backcountry boards in Joshua Tree National Park (this one is simply a bulletin board), is on your left, within only 50 yards of the campground entrance. Park there. The trailhead is immediately east of the board area. GPS: N34°04.49700' / W116°23.27520'

The Hike

As the mileage log below indicates, this is a very well-marked trail, both up Eureka Peak and down the California Riding & Hiking Trail return trip. In spite of that, there is a sense of wilderness excitement, because the hike to the peak gets out of the wash and into mountain canyons and ravines. Even with the intermittent signs, you can feel like an explorer.

The view from the peak is magnificent. The San Bernardinos, with their mantle of snow in winter and early spring, rise in the western distance. The park's ranges stretch away to the south and east. Although there is a road and parking area immediately downhill from the peak, it does not appear to be heavily used due to its distance from CA 62.

The return journey down the R & H track is the most heavily horse-used portion of this trail through the park. Elsewhere there is no trace of horse traffic. Here, trail signposts are almost unnecessary—just follow the hoofprints. Nevertheless, numerous arrow posts mark your way. There are, however, no mile markers as there are on the other sections. While signs on the higher section are nonexistent, the lower end of the trail sports painted, stenciled, and planted signposts verifying your location.

Descending the California Riding and Hiking Trail from Eureka Peak.

For a day trip close to populated Yucca Valley, this is the ideal outing. The exertion of the hike to the peak contrasts nicely with the relaxed stroll back down the wash via the Riding and Hiking Trail. The focus on wild mountains on the way up also contrasts with the views of the subdivisions of Yucca Valley on the way down.

Note: The Black Rock Canyon area has numerous hiking trails. A diagrammatic map is posted at the trailhead, or you can get one at the ranger station. These trails are signed. During the hike you will encounter numerous signposts. Most of these were put into place by volunteer equestrians. These are being replaced with etched metal signs by the park trail crew.

Miles and Directions

Note: The park plans to replace many of these signs.

0.0 From the trailhead, go east toward a nearby wash. The first 2-mile section of the Eureka Peak Trail coincides with the California Riding and Hiking Trail (Calif. R & H).

1.5 Ignore the junction with "FT." Stay left on the Calif. R & H over the saddle to the upper valley.

2.0 A junction clearly signposted EP marks the Eureka Peak Trail. Turn up the wash.

2.3 Disregard the junction with "SL." Continue in the well-traveled main wash as it climbs and narrows.

3.8 A comforting EP arrow is posted in the wash. Continue straight up the wash.

4.0 At the BF/EP signpost, follow the EP arrow to the right.

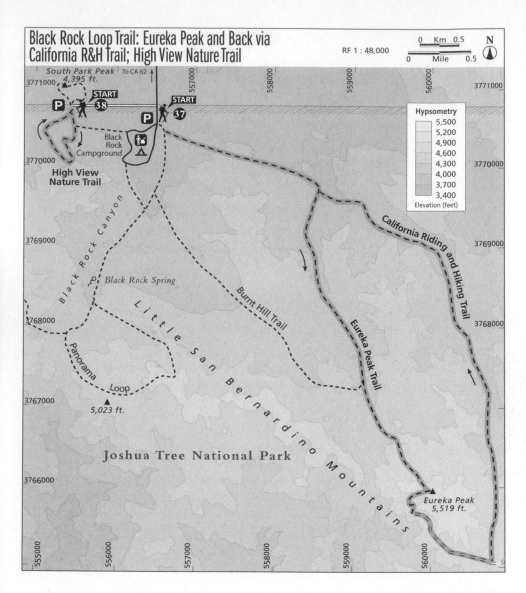

Black Rock Loop Trail: Eureka Peak and Back via
California R&H Trail; High View Nature Trail

RF 1 : 48,000

0   Km   0.5

0   Mile   0.5

N

Hypsometry

5,500
5,200
4,900
4,600
4,300
4,000
3,700
3,400
Elevation (feet)

South Park Peak 4,395 ft.

To CA 62

START 38

P

START 37

P

Black Rock Campground

High View Nature Trail

Black Rock Canyon

Black Rock Spring

Burnt Hill Trail

Little San Bernardino Mountains

Panorama Loop

5,023 ft.

Joshua Tree National Park

Eureka Peak Trail

California Riding and Hiking Trail

Eureka Peak 5,519 ft.

4.3 The EP/BH marker confirms you're on the correct trail as it becomes a twisting footpath up the ravine to the peak.

4.9 At the mountain ridge, turn left to the summit (0.1 mile), right to the parking area and Covington Road, which you'll take down to meet the Calif. R & H Trail for the hike back to Black Rock Campground.

5.2 At the parking area, turn left and take the road downhill to the Calif. R & H Trail.

5.7 Find the Calif. R & H Trail on your left in a valley before Covington Road begins climbing. A large brown and white sign is 30 yards off the road; what you will probably notice first is the house-shaped backcountry-regulations sign, which is only 10 yards off the road under a huge Joshua tree. Head north down the sloping wash.

8.5 Back at the original fork where you met the Eureka Peak Trail, continue on the Calif. R & H Trail back to the campground.

10.3 Watch for the left turn where the trail returns to the backcountry board and the wash (and the horse traffic); continue north. You can see the campground from here.

10.5 Arrive back at the backcountry board.

38 High View Nature Trail

Just west of the Black Rock Campground, this outing provides a lofty view of surrounding peaks and the sprawl nearby in Yucca Valley.

See map on page 108.
Start: 5 miles southeast of the town of Yucca Valley.
Distance: 1.3-mile loop.
Approximate hiking time: 0.5 to 2 hours.
Difficulty: Moderate.

Trail surface: Dirt path.
Seasons: October through May.
Maps: Trails Illustrated Joshua Tree National Park; USGS Yucca Valley South.
Trail contact: Joshua Tree National Park (see appendix D).

Finding the trailhead: From California Highway 62 in Yucca Valley, turn south on Avalon Avenue and drive 0.7 mile to where it becomes Palomar Drive. Continue on Palomar 2.3 miles to the left turn on Joshua Tree Lane. Take Joshua Tree Lane 1 mile to the T intersection at San Marino Avenue. Turn right and go 0.3 mile to Black Rock Road. Turn left on Black Rock and drive south 0.5 mile to the park entrance. Immediately before the entrance, turn right (west) onto a dirt road and go west 0.8 mile to the parking area. GPS: N34 4.579' / W116 23.966'

The Hike

This nature trail travels to the top of a hill, providing a view over the Yucca Valley and the eastern end of the park. There is a register at the summit, as well as a bench. The trail follows a relatively gentle route as it climbs 320 feet. Numbered sites line the trail; the brochures are available at the Black Rock Ranger Station in the adjacent campground.

If you're staying at the campground, a hilly but far more scenic route exists that connects the campground with the nature trail. It leaves from the top of the loop above the ranger station and enters the nature trail loop in its first section. Although it is clearly marked, this alternate route from the campground has an aura of wilderness. We spotted two coyotes hunting for rabbits in the middle of the afternoon on our loop hike from the campground.

Option: Heading north out of the parking area is a 0.8-mile loop trail to the top of South Park Peak. This gentle ascent lies outside of Joshua Tree National Park. It is part of the Yucca Valley Parks District.

Afterword

As seasoned hikers accustomed to the high snowy mountains of the Northern Rockies, we were excited when the idea of exploring some of the California desert was presented to us. It would be hard to find two more disparate regions—the California desert and the Northern Rockies—within the lower forty-eight. We viewed the opportunity to learn more about such a different ecosystem as a tremendous challenge. And we foresaw many interim challenges along the way, such as the challenge of truly getting to know this splendid country and its hidden treasures beyond the roads. There would be the challenges of climbing rugged peaks, of safely traversing vast expanses of open desert, of navigating across alluvial fans to secluded canyons, of learning enough about the interconnected web of desert geology, flora, and fauna to be able to interpret some of its wonders for others to appreciate. These beckoned to us from blank spots on the park map.

But we each face a far greater challenge: the challenge of wilderness stewardship, which must be shared by all who venture into the wilderness of Joshua Tree and California's other desert parks.

Wilderness stewardship can take many forms, from political advocacy to a zero-impact hiking and camping ethic to quietly setting the example of respect for wild country for others to follow. The political concessions that eventually brought about passage of the long-awaited California Desert Protection Act have been made. Boundaries were gerrymandered, exclusions made, and nonconforming uses grandfathered. Still, the park lines that have been drawn in this great park represent a tremendous step forward in the ongoing battle to save what little remains of our diminishing wilderness heritage.

But drawing lines is only the first step. Now, the great challenge is to take care of what we have. We can each demonstrate this care every time we set out on a hike. It comes down to respect for the untamed but fragile desert, for those wild creatures who have no place else to live, for other visitors, and for those yet unborn who will retrace our hikes into the next century and beyond.

We will be judged not by the mountains we climb but by what we pass on to others in an unimpaired condition. Happy hiking, and may your trails be clear with the wind and sun at your back.

Appendix A: Our Favorite Hikes

Open Desert

California Riding and Hiking Trail: Covington Flat to Keys View (36) Crosses varied terrain, includes side trip to Quail Peak

Canyon

Pine City/Canyon (25) Dramatic canyon with boulder scrambling

Oasis

Lost Palms Oasis (1) Remote oasis, largest palm grove in Joshua Tree National Park

Interpretive Nature Trail

Cottonwood Spring Nature Trail (4) Native American uses and processes for desert plants

Prehistory and History

Barker Dam Nature Trail Loop (32) Native American petroglyphs, ranching

Mines and Mills

Lost Horse Mine Loop (16) Well-preserved historic mine structures
Wall Street Mill (30) Gold-processing mill

Appendix B: Recommended Equipment

Use the following checklists as you assemble your gear for hiking the Joshua Tree National Park.

Day Hike

❏ sturdy, well-broken-in, light- to medium-weight hiking boots
   broad-brimmed hat, which must be windproof
❏ long-sleeved shirt for sun protection
❏ long pants for protection against sun and brush
❏ water: two quarts to one gallon/day (depending on season), in sturdy screw-top plastic containers
❏ large-scale topo map and compass (adjusted for magnetic declination)
❏ whistle, mirror, and matches (for emergency signals)
❏ flashlight (in case your hike takes longer than you expect)
❏ sunblock and lip sunscreen
❏ insect repellent (in season)
❏ pocketknife
❏ small first-aid kit: tweezers, bandages, antiseptic, moleskin, snakebite extractor kit
❏ bee sting kit (over-the-counter antihistamine or epinephrine by prescription) as needed for the season
❏ windbreaker (or rain gear in season)
❏ lunch or snack, with baggie for your trash
❏ toilet paper, with a plastic zipper bag to pack it out
❏ your FalconGuide

Optional gear
❏ camera and film
❏ binoculars
❏ bird and plant guidebooks
❏ notebook and pen/pencil

Winter High-Country Trips

All of the above, plus:
❏ gaiters
❏ warm ski-type hat and gloves
❏ warm jacket

Backpacking Trips/Overnights

All of the above, plus:
- ❏ backpack (internal or external frame)
- ❏ more water (at least a gallon a day, plus extra for cooking—cache or carry)
- ❏ clothing for the season
- ❏ sleeping bag and pad
- ❏ tent with fly
- ❏ toiletries
- ❏ stove with fuel bottle and repair kit
- ❏ pot, bowl, cup, and eating utensils
- ❏ food (freeze-dried meals require extra water)
- ❏ water filter designed and approved for backcountry use (if the route passes a water source)
- ❏ nylon cord (50 to 100 feet for hanging food, drying clothes, etc.)
- ❏ additional plastic bags for carrying out trash

Appendix C: Other Information Sources and Maps

Natural History Association

Joshua Tree National Park Association
74485 National Park Drive
Twentynine Palms, CA 92277
(760) 367–5535
Website: www.joshuatree.org

The association is a nonprofit membership organization dedicated to the preservation and interpretation of the natural and human history of the park. Membership benefits include book discounts, educational programs, and periodic newsletters.

Map Sources

Joshua Tree National Park topographic backcountry and hiking map, 1:78,125 scale, published by National Geographic Trails Illustrated. This map is available from the Joshua Tree National Park Association bookstores at the park, from many outdoor shops, and also directly from National Geographic, https://www.natgeomaps.com/trail-maps/trails-illustrated-maps.

USGS topographic maps are available from https://store.usgs.gov/maps. Printed copies can be ordered, or PSF files can be downloaded for free.

There are many online mapping programs and apps that seamlessly integrate USGS topo maps, the digital National Map, as well as satellite imagery. One such site is GaiaGPS.com, https://www.gaiagps.com, which also features Trail Illustrated maps and many other map layers. Gaia GPS has GPS waypoint and route tools, and tracks and waypoints that you record on your smartphone are automatically saved to the Gaia cloud and appear on the GaiaGPS web page. You'll need a paid subscription to use all the features (which is true of most online mapping programs), but the cost is far cheaper than printed USGS topo maps.

Appendix D: Park Management Agencies

Superintendent
Joshua Tree National Park
74485 National Park Drive
Twentynine Palms, CA 92277-3597
(760) 367–5500
Website: www.nps.gov/jotr

For information about wilderness and other public lands adjacent to the park, contact:
Bureau of Land Management
California Desert District
22835 Calle San Juan De Los Lagos
Moreno Valley, CA 92553
(951) 697–5200
Website: https://www.blm.gov/california

Index

About the Authors

Polly and **Bill Cunningham** are married partners on the long trail of life. Polly, formerly a history teacher in St. Louis, Missouri, now makes her home with Bill in Choteau, Montana. She is pursuing multiple careers as a freelance writer and wilderness guide and working with the elderly. Polly has hiked and backpacked extensively throughout many parts of the country.

Bill is a lifelong "Wildernut," as a conservation activist, backpacking outfitter, and former wilderness field studies instructor. During the 1970s and 1980s he was a field rep for The Wilderness Society and Montana Wilderness Association. Bill has written several books, including *Wild Montana*, published by Falcon Press in 1995, plus numerous articles about wilderness areas based on his extensive personal exploration.

In addition to *Hiking Joshua Tree National Park*, Polly and Bill have coauthored several other FalconGuide books, including *Wild Utah* (1998), *Hiking New Mexico's Gila Wilderness* (1999), *Hiking New Mexico's Aldo Leopold Wilderness* (2002), and *Hiking California's Desert Parks* (2006).

Decades ago both Bill and Polly lived in California close to the desert—Bill in Bakersfield and Polly in San Diego. They enjoyed renewing their ties with California while exploring Joshua Tree National Park for this book. Months of driving, camping, and hiking, with laptop and camera, have increased their enthusiasm for California's desert wilderness. They want others to have as much fun exploring this fabulously wide-open country as they did.

Authors Polly and Bill Cunningham

Bruce Grubbs is an avid camper, backpacker, hiker, mountain biker, and cross-country skier who has been exploring the American desert for more than thirty years. A professional outdoor writer and photographer, he has written many previous FalconGuides, including *Hiking Arizona*. He lives in Flagstaff, Arizona.